Moving Mountains

Moving Mountains

MY UNLIKELY JOURNEY FROM EXTREME HARDSHIP AND POVERTY IN MAO'S CHINA TO OPPORTUNITY AND SUCCESS IN THE USA

BY

BRIAN CHANG

IRON MAN PRESS
Minneapolis, Minnesota

Copyright © 2024 Rene & Brian Chang

All rights reserved.
No part of this publication, or parts thereof, may be reproduced in any form without the written permission of the publisher.

Library of Congress Control Number: 2024907545
Chang, Brian, author.
Chang, Rene, editor.
MOVING MOUNTAINS / Brian Chang
ISBN: 978-1-7379536-4-7

Move Mountains poem used with poet's permission.

IRON MAN PRESS
Minneapolis, Minnesota

THIS BOOK IS LOVINGLY DEDICATED TO

Rene Wyman Chang,
my loving wife, friend, and partner since 1996

Natalie and Melanie Chang,
my beloved, God-sent daughters

Yu-Lan Zhu and Zi-Zhen Chang,
my forever kind, adoring, and beloved parents

Contents

Part One 1

Chapter I - Urban to Rural life 3

Chapter II - My Parents and Family Life 15

Chapter III - Life On The Farm. 27

Chapter IV - My Education. 47

Chapter V - Hope 63

Chapter VI - College and Heartbreak 77

Chapter VII - Leaving China 97

Chapter VIII - Culture Shock and Sorrow 121

Chapter IX - Finding Love 145

Part Two 155

Chapter X - Adventures in International Business 157

Chapter XI - Moving to China and Lessons Learned. . . 179

Afterword 188

Acknowledgments. 193

Preface

I have lived a fantastical life, almost
far-fetched in both misfortune and unimaginable good
fortune. For years I have sought to tell this story, which
is actually two stories: first, my emotional journey
out of China, and second, my ongoing
and prosperous work with
and within China.

Please read this book knowing,
as Confucius once taught:
words are the voice of the heart.

Part One:
My Journey From China

Traveling to Machu Picchu is a challenge, but it was on my list of things to do in my life. So, in June of 2022, I flew with my younger daughter, Melanie, to Lima, Peru, then on to Cusco. Following the flight, we took a two-hour bus ride, then a ninety-minute train ride, both moving at no more than twenty miles per hour to reach our destination.

I did not anticipate what would happen on the train ride to Machu Picchu, during the eerily slow climb up the mountain on a single track. Suddenly I felt myself on a different train forty-seven years earlier, traveling at that same, unnervingly slow speed away from the northern metropolis of Tianjin, where I was born and raised, to the mountainous village in northern China where I was expected to spend the rest of my life as a peasant farmer under Mao's Cultural Revolution.

I was eighteen then, and I felt my life was over.

On that trip, I had no hope for myself against the brutal reality of a Communist regime. On this trip decades later, I was a free man with many resources, the ability to choose my pathways in life, and to visit an ancient wonder in the Peruvian mountains with my daughter.

Imagine the emotions stirring within me as I thought of my life journey thus far, and the years and travels that took me from that moment to this. Far-fetched? Yes. Grateful? Absolutely. Archaeology indicates that those who lived in Machu Picchu hundreds of years ago were immigrants to the area. They traveled to their destination seeking something, though exactly what we will never know.

But I always knew why I traveled.

My determination began with that slow ride up the mountain from Tianjin.

CHAPTER I

URBAN TO RURAL LIFE
FROM TIANJIN TO CHENG VILLAGE

Summer 1975

I lost my urban residency in July 1975 when I was eighteen years old. My registration, or *hukou*, was revoked according to the Rules for Households Registration set forth by Mao during the Communist Regime. What did that mean to me? Once I was sent away to the countryside, I would not be able to return as a city resident. Once registered as a rural citizen, I would lose all my urban benefits. This meant no food rations, no job, no way to survive. No urban resident would want to marry me with a rural registration. As early as the late 1950s, Mao began calling urban youth to live and work in the villages of mountainous rural areas. At first, people were naive and went to the farms willingly. By the time I graduated from high school and was sent to the farm, we were all aware of the hardships that awaited us in the countryside: the primitive conditions, the lack of running water and electricity, the abuse of young females, work without purpose, draconian punishments, and crushing despair. Nobody wanted to go to the farm anymore.

Mao's policy required educated youth—those who had completed middle or high school or college in urban areas—to relocate to rural parts of China and work on farms, to be "reeducated" by the peasants and farmers who had, at best, only six years of compulsory education. At the time

China was predominantly an agricultural country, and illiteracy was rampant. In addition, the economy was on the brink of collapse, and young people who completed nine or twelve years of schooling in the city had no job prospects. The government feared that they could easily fall into rebellion and troublemaking. Educated youth were promised future leadership positions in the rural communities. "You want to grow roots there, become a leader, and enrich the life of the countryside," we were told.

Earlier in the Cultural Revolution, Red Guards, or *Hong Wei Bing*, played a major role in following Mao's directive to "destroy the old world," causing irreparable damage to the country's heritage and culture, including the physical destruction of valuable relics. In 1967, the relocation of these Revolutionary Young Warriors to remote areas seemed a clever way to dismantle this "destructive" force. They, too, were sent to the countryside.

By 1975, family planning measures were already in place to encourage reducing family size and the population in general. If a family had two children, one would be "encouraged" to go to a rural area after finishing middle or high school, and the other would be assigned a job in the city. Only one child in a family of three children would be sent to the farm, but in a family of four like mine, two of us would be expected to go. The best urban jobs were in government agencies because workers never got fired, and there was little actual work to do, as they were considered positions of power and privilege. Workers also preferred jobs in state-owned companies because they always got paid regardless of the workload and enjoyed "the iron bowl" of security. But even the lowest and least desirable urban jobs were better than leaving the city to work on a farm.

Each family in China had a roughly bound book, known as the *hukou*, or the book of household registration, which included one page for each family member, stating the individual's name and date of birth. Because the literal meaning of *kou* is "mouth," each family member was considered a mouth to feed. Pages in the book were bound by a cloth ribbon strung through three holes tying them together, and this information formed the basis for all rations—food, cotton, cloth, grain, coal—any supplies required for survival.

These pages also determined where you could live. If you were registered in the *hukou* as an urban citizen, you were allowed to live in the city. The *hukou* system in China meant that wherever you were born, you remained. If you were born in Shanghai, you were lucky and could spend the rest of your life there. But if you were born a peasant in a rural area, you were destined to live in the countryside for the remainder of your life. When educated youth were changed from urban to rural registration, their pages were physically removed from the book, and went with them to the farm, where they instantly became rural residents. Consequently, they were denied food rations—rural residents ate and consumed only what they could grow and produce. This stark difference was a source of culture shock to us ex-urbanites.

When I finished middle school, I made the decision to attend high school knowing that while I was in high school, my oldest sister, Tieying, would graduate from middle school and be assigned an urban job. We had numerous family discussions about this situation. My parents did not want me to leave and relinquish my urban status, as I was their only son, and according to the unspoken Chinese social security system, I would be the one in the family expected to care for my parents as they aged. My sisters would find husbands and care for their husbands' parents. This was how the filial piety system worked in China, and that has not changed. In those days, there were no nursing homes or assisted-living facilities. The sons were their elderly parents' only caregivers.

I had already decided I would be the one to go to the farm, but I did not want to make it easy on the officials who sought to "persuade" me. I decided I would bargain with them to ensure urban citizenship for my middle sister, Tierong. Government representatives at that time used cajolery and coercive sessions to subdue people into capitulation. (This ritual is still practiced whenever the government needs its citizens to cooperate.) Each session might last up to three hours, but could continue with another session, back-to-back and all night. Teams of officials lectured about the future, and the peasants who needed us and other falsehoods, badgering until the family was so exhausted and humiliated, they literally handed over the *hukou* book for the child's page to be removed.

After enduring two weeks of daily "persuasion" sessions, I was finally able to negotiate written assurance with the government representatives that I would be the one from my family to serve in the countryside, if my second sister could remain in the city. By the time my youngest sister, Tiewei, finished middle school, Mao had died, and the relocation program had mostly died with him, as nobody else had the fortitude to enforce it. But that was later.

On a late summer morning in 1975, I reported to the Tianjin train station, along with some 1,200 other educated youth, all of us about to travel together for work on designated farms in ninety different villages, part of Mao's nearly ten-year "climb up the mountain and settle down into the village" movement. Officially called *cha dui luo hu*, it translates literally into "re-establish residence" or *hukou* by joining a rural community brigade. There was no choice. Mao's "settle down into the village" reeducation plan forced a total of twenty million youth like me to surrender their urban residencies and settle into rural or collective farming communities. As the slogan stated, we were expected to grow roots and never leave.

Everyone's family members and relatives arrived at the train station that day to bid us farewell. We all believed that we would never return as residents of Tianjin again. Because very few traveled in those days, watching a loved one get on a long-distance train was anomalous. Everyone wanted to participate in our send-off. My parents, childhood friends, my uncle, and many cousins came to see me off. It had the surreal mood of a funeral. Each traveler was given a pair of army green rubber shoes and a red and white enamel basin, designed with images of Mao's smiling face or a large flower suggesting a happy occasion. A government official shouted into a megaphone across the crowd, disingenuously telling us how brave and glorious we were, doing our patriotic duty to change the countryside to make it better for everyone, but no one paid attention. All garbage. Nobody listened to him.

More than ten thousand people gathered that day at the train station. Suddenly someone in this vast crowd started weeping, not very loud, but loud enough for everyone to hear that one soft sob in those thousands of people. Then another sobbed, and ten more, and others began crying, this wave of sorrow continuing for only a few minutes, but seeming to last forever. Even the speaker, who must have been a parent himself, looked moved. We all felt a heavy, lingering cloud of gloom. There was such despair.

Soon it was time to board the train. People did not hug in those days, as it was not the custom. We waved a prolonged goodbye as an entertainer sang songs praising Mao and a drum band played. Then the steam engines fired up, the loud whistle blowing several times as we pulled out of the station, away from our parents, our relatives, our city, and the civilization we knew. When I looked out the train window, I saw that my mother had turned her head the other way so I would not see her crying. My father's gaze remained steady, his eyes fixed on me until he was out of sight. My sisters did not completely understand the significance of my leaving. We had eaten dumplings the night before to mark my departure, so they thought it was a type of celebration. As they watched the train depart, I do not believe they experienced the same overwhelming emotion as my parents. I can imagine, then and now, the helplessness, and even the guilt they felt. As a father of two loving daughters, I would do anything to protect them and prevent them from any harm. But my parents had no option.

We traveled slowly north from Tianjin for six hours, to our destination of Ji Zhou County, as it is called today. Once we were out of the city, peasants boarded the train, too, many carrying small animals like chickens and piglets. The train was hot even though the windows were open, and the mood was tense. Most of the men on the train smoked, which filled the train cars much like the heavy cloud of dread we felt. Those of us assigned to Cheng Village rode together in the same section, but we had little to say as we faced the unknown. We sat alert, waiting. A voice through the train loudspeaker incessantly blasted propaganda as we moved northward, playing revolutionary songs based on Mao's poems with words like "demonstrate your talent in the countryside, the countryside is wide, opportunities are endless, reeducation from peasants will temper you to be solid Communist successors, more qualified to carry on the revolutionary cause and the red flag, our symbol of martyrs' blood." That loudspeaker did not leave us in silence for one minute. At some point in our journey, we asked the conductor to please shut off that voice, but he could only turn down the volume. He claimed to "lack the authority" to turn it off. The noise continued to the point of torture.

Thirteen of us, seven boys and six girls, were assigned to Cheng Village, a community of 1,500 people divided into four "brigades." Each brigade was split into four quadrants based on geography: the northeast and northwest sub-brigades and the southeast and southwest sub-brigades. The Communist government has always reveled in using military-style hierarchy and terminology—anything to tighten the grasp on their control. In our group of thirteen, three of us came from the same high school, but not the same class. The rest were all strangers, meeting for the first time on this train ride.

Little conversation took place as we traveled. What was there to say? The only certainty about our future was the hardship that awaited us and the anguish of leaving our families behind. Compounding my grief was the belief that I was no longer useful to my parents and not able to help them or contribute to their well-being. I felt defeated.

One of the boys assigned to my village, named Lu, was a little older than the rest of us because he had escaped rural assignment for two years, using his overall poor and weak health to obtain stamped certificates of exemption from the doctor. By the summer of 1975, when the authorities conducted their "recruitment" campaigns, Lu was no longer able to convince them that he was still unfit to serve. I met Lu on the train ride out of Tianjin when he offered me a cigarette. He was a chain-smoker, thin, pale, and unhealthy in appearance. We called him Little Lu. When I asked what year he had finished school, he replied "Seventy-three," explaining that he had not been well enough to go to the farm for the past two years. "So you are well now?" I asked. He said no, but he failed to convince the authorities this time. Then with a grin he added, "And I was tired of living off my parents."

When the train arrived at the township station, one hundred of us got off to continue our journeys to various villages. The party secretary of Cheng Village, Jian-hua Xu, met us with two carts, each pulled by two horses, with separate carts for men and women. We drove through the seat of the township on rough dirt roads made worse by recent rains. As the cart moved along, we bounced and slid on the hard, wooden benches, this being the primary, even luxury, mode of transportation in the countryside in 1975. The horses had trouble navigating the ruts, though the drivers, who did this as a profession, took care to protect their carts and horses from damage. Our driver asked, "Have you ever been on a cart like this?" When we all answered no, he replied, "Then this will be a good experience for you!" We rode for another two and a half hours before arriving at our destination.

Then there we were. Villagers gathered around us, staring and pointing. Most of them had never seen anyone from the city, nor anyone wearing accessorized silk scarves or plastic-soled, factory-made shoes.

I had a small family trunk with me—a wooden box about two feet long by one foot wide and one foot deep—containing the few possessions given to me by my parents: an army shirt from a distant relative, an extra pair of shoes my mother had painstakingly stitched for me, a quilt for the bed or *kang,* as we called it, and an enamel mug for hot water. This trunk was stored alongside the *kang* in the bungalow where I lived on the farm. In China, a built-in bed filling half the room was known as a *kang,* or more specifically *yi jian wu zi, ban jian kang,* which literally means one bedroom with half the room being a bed. I slept on a *kang* both at my home in Tianjin and again while living on the farm.

Everything was primitive. Electricity was only available after midnight to be used exclusively for industrial purposes, like powering the pumps and grain-grinding machines, but not to light homes. Only the Communist Party leader had an electric light in his house, which was necessary, so they said, for him to conduct official business.

The thirteen of us ex-urbanites lived in a compound built specifically for our group that had also been wired for electricity. Our building housed the village office and included a study room and a loudspeaker system for official announcements. Despite this, there was no electrical lighting in our rooms. By 1975, farmers only reluctantly accepted educated youth. They did not need extra help in the fields, and they surely had no desire to feed any extra mouths with what little food they produced. We did not want to be on the farm, and the farmers did not want us there. The whole concept was absurd, and everyone suffered. The government gave the village 500 *yuan* per person to build the compound and to cover the settling and living expenses of the educated youth, which was supposed to appease the farmers.

During the first few months, our water came from a creek a quarter mile from our bungalow. It wasn't totally pristine, but at least it was fresh. Some farm families had wells, and within months, the village authority used the settlement funding to dig a well inside our compound.

Our group lived in one bungalow, which was subdivided into four rooms, with two bedrooms on each end and a common area in between. The girls were in two rooms on one side of the common area and the boys in the two rooms on the other side. We slept three or four to a *kang,* which was stationary, made of bricks built into the floor, and connected by a platform for sleeping. Each room had a wood-burning stove that connected to the *kang* and vented out under the beds and up through a chimney, providing the only heat we had in winter.

The stoves were also constructed of bricks and clay with built-in steel woks for cooking. They were fueled mostly with corn straw, not coal, as those in the city, and initially, none of us knew how to build a long-lasting fire without using more straw than was necessary for our allotment. We didn't feel the cold when we first arrived because it was late summer, but in the winter temperatures rarely went above freezing. The urine in the night pot froze every night, and we avoided using the outdoor toilet at any cost.

The first winter was arduous. Mao's dictates meant that no one could be idle, but frozen land could not be farmed in the winter, so our orders were to build a canal—despite the lack of any water source in that location. Each day we were required to chisel out one cubic meter per person, or roughly nine cubic feet, then we would carry the dirt and mud up the side of the canal using two wooden pails balanced at either end of a bamboo pole secured by hemp rope. This method, along with a wheelbarrow, is how we carried every material on the farm—water, food, manure, grain, anything. To maintain balance, we shifted the load from one shoulder to another as we carried the pails. The weight of the material we carried was often more than what we weighed, and the poles dug painfully into our shoulders. At night we slept on the bank of the canal to avoid wasting time going back and forth to our bungalow. It was impossible to warm up. Worse, the work was futile and totally unproductive.

Thus began my life as a rural resident.

CHAPTER II

MY PARENTS AND FAMILY LIFE
SHANDONG PROVINCE TO TIANJIN

1921 – 1975

My father, Zi-Zhen Chang, was an intelligent man. He was born in Shandong province in 1921 and was educated for five years in a Confucius-style village school, where he learned to calculate proficiently on an abacus and write beautiful calligraphy with a brush pen. The teachers in such schools did not expect to become rich; they were satisfied to be paid in grain and able to exist without having to work in the fields. My father had the misfortune to live in a village overcome by famine, so as a young man, he made his way north, the way many from rural villages did, walking toward Manchuria in Northeastern China, where the land was more fertile and poverty not as prevalent. He did what others did in that situation, begging alongside the road from one city to the next.

The country had become the Republic of China in 1911. During much of my father's childhood, various factions vied to control China, leaving the farmers on their own to survive as best they could. Village heads were appointed, but there was no organization or infrastructure, and no taxes. People lived freely but were also free to starve when times became difficult. These grim times created the vacuum that would later allow Mao to swoop in and denounce the past, vowing to grant land to the peasants with the promise of a better life.

As my father passed through the port city of Tianjin, still one of the largest cities in China, a man recognized my father's dialect. This was unusual and significant, because there were so many dialects in the country that even people living on two sides of the same narrow stream might speak differently. Those using the same dialect tended to trust one another, and even more so the farther they were from home. This man, Xu San Ye, owned and operated a large import-export business and enjoyed considerable wealth. He offered my father a place to live and a job in Tianjin, working for him as a domestic helper. When Mr. Xu discovered my father's skills with numbers and writing, he promoted him to a professional accounting position in his company.

My father was introduced to my mother by a relative—I never learned who—and they married the same day they met. They were both attractive people, my mother slightly taller than my father and warm and soft-hearted. Although they did not know each other when they married, I believe they came to love one another. I never heard them argue and always sensed a deep affection between them.

My mother, Yu-Lan Zhu, was beautiful, both inside and out. She came from a family of eight and grew up in the era when public education was not available, certainly not for girls from poor families; as such, she did not learn to read or write like my father. But she had a talent for numerous tasks and was always kind and gracious. When the Communist government began its "Get Rid of Illiteracy" campaign in the early 1950s—everything was a campaign—she took some night school classes, all mostly propaganda for the Communist Party, but she learned how to write her name. More important was my mother's natural way of reaching out to others by giving a bit of food to an elderly neighbor and always treating people with kindness.

My father was doing well until the Communist Party won the civil war against the Nationalists in 1949. Before that, my parents had enough to eat, even enough for my mother to help other members of her large family who were not faring as well. During his tenure at Mr. Xu's import-export company, my father worked hard at his job and did not complain. As luck would have it, he was drafted as an accountant for the Nationalists' military, but when the Nationalist Army lost to the Communist Army, my father found himself working for the wrong side. He was labeled a hard-evidence enemy—a Historical Counter Revolutionary to be exact—and demoted to a salary that was barely subsistence level. He earned sixty-two Chinese *yuan* a month (about U.S. $25 in the 1950s), which was slightly above the poverty level for a family of six, but just short of qualifying for any government assistance. When the Cultural Revolution started, he was further demoted from his accounting position to a job cleaning public toilets. The stench of the public toilet house could be washed off, but it was much more difficult to wash off the daily public humiliation my father suffered during those two years.

There were always multiple ways to be labeled an "enemy of the people" under Communist rule, including, but not limited to, these groups:

Landlord—anyone who owned and leased land; this later included factory owners, who were labeled Capitalists.
Rich Farmers—any farmer who hired help.
Counterrevolutionaries—anyone opposing the government in any manner.
Bad Elements—a general category for anyone the government chose to dislike for any arbitrary reason.

Rightists—anyone with bourgeois leanings, including those wearing leather shoes or eating foreign foods, like bread and butter.

Over time additional categories like these were identified as "enemies of the people":

Counterrevolutionary Experts—including scientists, magicians, even comedians and chefs.
Counterrevolutionary Intellectuals—professors and teachers who voiced their opinions that ran counter to government propaganda.

By the time I was born, my parents lived in a one-room bungalow in a row of other one-room apartments just like ours, without plumbing or running water, which they rented from the government for roughly 3 percent of my father's monthly income. The government owned all real estate property at the time. The room measured 120 square feet with one door and one small window alongside the door. This room contained everything we owned and provided shelter for everything we did. It was where we slept, cooked, ate, studied, and entertained. It was both our storage room and where we washed our bodies and our clothes. It was also where we kept the used water and sewage that we carried outside and disposed of in a common sewage area.

All six family members slept on the same *kang*, made of stacked bricks on each end supporting a sheet of plywood that was high enough to provide storage space below. Every winter we constructed a new "chimney" out of an aluminum pipe inserted through a windowpane to vent the fumes from the coal-burning stove which provided our heat in the winter. This was somewhat different than the stationary *kang* I slept on later when I lived in the village. At night, my parents would sleep in the middle, with my three sisters next to my mother and me next to my father. My mother made quilts by hand with scraps of fabric, which covered us in cold weather. During the day, we folded the quilts neatly and stacked them in one corner of the bed on top of the small storage chest where we kept our few possessions. We owned so little. I had one shirt that my mother washed every Sunday after I went to bed. She patched it whenever it tore or wore thin, and turned the collar inside out when one side was threadbare. Every shirt I had in childhood was patched in at least four places, which always included the elbows. (Years later in the United States, I was stunned to discover that patched elbow jackets were considered fashionable.) To celebrate Lunar New Year, my mother would give me a new shirt and a new pair of shoes to last throughout the next year.

The new year holiday is pivotal in Chinese life, marking endings and beginnings, honoring ancestors, family, and home. Just before the holiday began, we thoroughly cleaned our house. We moved everything we owned outside, then mopped the floors until the cement literally shone. We washed the glass windowpanes and beat the dust and dirt out of our quilts with a rolling pin. We then scrubbed all three layers of the quilts—the top and bottom and the cotton batting between them— dunking them in a bucket and using a washboard, then dried each layer and put the quilts back together, adding new cotton batting. This endeavor took an entire week and involved the whole family. We called this our spring cleaning, and all people, no matter how poor, performed the ritual house cleaning. During the holiday, we rode a trolley to visit my maternal grandmother who lived about three miles away. My maternal grandfather had died by then. Because my father's family lived 300 miles away, we had neither the time nor money to visit them. I was told that both of my paternal grandparents passed away before I was born. As a child, I only got to know my maternal grandmother. To this day I wonder about the lives of my other three grandparents.

Although we barely had enough to eat, my mother always made it a magical Lunar New Year's celebration. With very few resources, she crafted steamed dumplings in a special wooden mold and decorated them with smiling faces. She washed Chinese pennies, then buried them in six of the boiling dumplings, hoping that each of her children would choose one or two dumplings with the hidden coin. Legend had it that those who got a penny dumpling would "strike it rich" or at least have a chance at becoming affluent in the New Year. If we did not finish eating all the dumplings, she coaxed us to continue, wanting all of us—especially me, her only son—to find a coin or two. In the first minute of the new year, we would light a bundle of 100 firecrackers to welcome the new year and to scare away any demons or malevolent spirits threatening to harm us. As the only son, I was charged with lighting the firecrackers.

Debt was not only discouraged but was—and still is—considered shameful in Chinese culture. As such, even in the most desperate of times, borrowing money has never been in my nature. I disapproved of the idea, even as an eight-year-old boy. To celebrate the lunar holiday one year, my mother made dumplings with pork, and one of the neighbor boys jeered that the only reason we had pork was because his mother had lent my mother two *yuan* to buy it. I was furious and refused to eat the dumplings. I apologized to my mother later, but at the time, I believed it was so wrong. You do not consume what you do not own.

Looking back, I wonder how my mother managed to make the holiday festive for her children when we were so impoverished that mere survival was difficult. We always ate meals on a low, five-inch-tall table placed on top of the bed. There we also chopped vegetables, kneaded the bread dough, and did all our food preparation. When we ate, four of us sat on top of the bed and the other two in chairs on the side of the bed. Each of us had only one bowl. There were no extra bowls or dishes of any kind, so breaking a bowl created a hardship. We also did our homework on the bed, or *kang*. My mother made quilts and cotton pants and coats, all on the bed.

Our coal-burning stove was stored outside next to the door for about nine months of the year. When we brought it inside the house for the winter, we removed a windowpane to vent the smoke and carbon monoxide through a narrow pipe which heated the room at the same time. Each day we made a stove fire of newspaper, twigs, and coal. There was an art to making it last because we were not able to cook if the fire extinguished. One twenty-five-watt light bulb lit the room when it was dark. It was the only device in our house that used electricity. The few dishes and utensils we owned were stored in a cabinet in the corner of the room. There was a mechanical clock on the table, which we wound every night, and a large wooden basin for washing our clothes, our quilts, and our bodies. We used a smaller porcelain basin for washing faces and feet and another just for our dishes.

When my sisters and mother washed themselves or changed clothes, my father and I stepped outside to protect their modesty. Other than hanging a curtain around the bed, we had little separation or privacy from each other in any way. It was impossible to take a full bath in our one-room apartment. During my childhood, I never took a full bath. People who had money routinely used public bathhouses, but it was not affordable for a family like ours. Taking a full bath at a public bathhouse was always a special treat and was usually done right before the Chinese New Year holiday. During the summer months, the Hai River, which runs through Tianjin, became a popular, though dangerous, bathhouse for many people. It was there I learned how to swim and often bathed and showered, but I never told my parents. They had forbidden me to go to the Hai River because people drowned every day, the undercurrents were so strong.

Running water came from a community pipe outside, sewage was emptied at a community drain, and the toilet was a communal house two blocks away. In my childhood, the communal bathroom offered no privacy, no walls or dividers, no water, no soap or paper towels, no ventilation, and never and nowhere the luxury of private space. When I learned that parents in this country punish their children by sending them to their bedrooms, I could not believe it. How can this be a punishment, to have a room all to yourself, doing whatever you please?

If we wanted boiling water for tea, we went to a boiler house, and for two pennies we could fill a large thermos. Summer nights were so hot that my father and I slept outside on the street, along with other men and boys, setting down mats and enduring relentless biting mosquitoes.

We found ingenious ways to obtain more supplies and food that we needed to survive. By the age of seven, I learned to linger in the area where the residents picked up their vegetable rations, and waited for cabbage leaves to fall to the ground as people rode home on their bicycles. I also retrieved leftover bits of coal that were being discarded. I went to the factory boilers and, using a stick to avoid burning my fingers, I would scoop up the coal that was not fully consumed, place it on a screen to shake off the dust and debris, and take it home. When we had gathered enough of these remnants, my father and I would pound them into powder to mix with clay and water, then form the mixture into balls and dry them in the sun. In this way, my father and I created new coal balls to burn in the stove.

My mother handmade everything we wore, and everything was used and reused. To craft our shoes, she cut rags into between ten and twenty layers for each sole. She then glued the layers together with corn paste and dried them in the sun. Once dried, my mother carefully cut and patterned intricate stitches to hold them in place. It took her two weeks just to make the soles. The top of the shoe was made of corduroy, which she bought with a few pennies at the fabric store. Through his work my father received coupons to purchase leather shoes. At that time in China, everything was rationed, not just food. Shoes, bikes, radios, watches, sugar, and cigarettes, even medicine, required a certificate plus the money to purchase. Because it would have been impossible for my father to come up with enough money to buy leather shoes, he gave his hard-earned shoe coupon to a friend.

The only time my father ever spanked me was when I came home with my new shoes covered in mud. I was seven years old. "Don't you understand," he said to me, "how hard your mother works to make your shoes?" I still weep when I think of that incident, the idea that I had somehow offended my mother by not respecting her efforts. After that I never wore my shoes in bad weather. If it rained or snowed making the ground muddy and wet, I removed my shoes and walked home barefoot.

Food was strictly rationed during the Cultural Revolution. Our family of six qualified for only so much grain, so many sweet potatoes and cabbage, and just one kilo of meat to last an entire month. These rations were calculated according to government guidelines, based not only on the number of members per household, but also on each person's age. Because the allotted rations were never adequate, we were always hungry. The lack of food was not a problem unique to our family. Millions of people went hungry each month. Consequently, the government introduced a "borrow your ration from the following month" program for us urban residents. As a result, on the twenty-fifth of each month, lines formed in front of the Grain Store at five in the morning, even though the store did not open until eight. If we arrived any later, all the grain might be gone. I stood in line many times for my family, often bringing my Chinese language book to read or recite while waiting.

I went to bed hungry every night with rare exception, and to this day I still have a sense of food insecurity. I am nicknamed "the food police" at my house. I never waste food, and obsessively check the refrigerator and freezer to make sure no perfectly good food has been thrown away just because it has an expiration date. We must use everything—I make sure of it. I cannot help myself.

I did not go to the countryside unfamiliar with deprivation and difficulty. But there I met a level of hardship even worse than what I had experienced at home.

CHAPTER III

LIFE ON THE FARM
CHENG VILLAGE

1975 – 1976

Cheng Village was one of about twenty under the administration of You Gu Zhuang township, which had a population of about 27,000 and covered approximately twenty-five square kilometers of land. Cheng Village was then, and is now, one of the larger villages, which was why it was divided into four sub-brigades. There were no paved roads, no running water, and no sewage, with electricity reserved only for industrial use. The whole township shared one small hospital, one restaurant, and one state-owned, co-op department store that sold everything the farmers could not produce themselves, from sponge cake to kerosene lamps. The township had a middle school, but no high school. The main source of entertainment tended to be gossip, as there was no library or cinema nor entertainment of any kind. Everyone knew everything; there were no secrets.

Every morning roosters on the farm would crow their wake-up call. For breakfast, we usually ate corn or millet porridge and a pickled turnip for the salt. We grew huge turnips, as wide as grapefruits and about twelve inches long, and stored them in a brine of salt and water. It did not take us long to learn how to preserve and store them for the winter, when there were very few vegetables available. During the summer months, we often made a kind of bread out of wheat flour, which made the best breakfast. Unfortunately, the rest of the year only sorghum flour was available. Mao preferred sorghum because it was easy to grow and produced high yields. Never mind that it tastes bitter and is difficult to cook and digest. The government desired higher yields of agricultural products than those produced in the U.S., so to them it was a competition. As such, local officials focused on increasing yields by growing easy crops, regardless of demand, quality, or taste.

Most of the year we returned to the bungalow for a lunch of corn, steamed yam, or pumpkin soup, but during harvest we dined in the field, where we were each brought two pieces of steamed bread prepared with good grain, onions, and oil. This lunch sustained us until the evening's dinner of millet and rice with stir-fried vegetables, like green beans, cabbage, or squash.

During the first twelve months at Cheng Village, our group of thirteen shared a ration of two kilos of pork each month, which we saved for special dinners, harvesting, or spring planting, when physical strength was required. When we made dumplings, we would work together to make enough for each of us to have a bowl of sixty—so many dumplings that we would be stuffed after eating them. But I remember always continuing to eat. It was the one time I did not feel hungry after a meal, and I discovered that my stomach could adjust to being unusually full on these special occasions. Sometimes we would make noodles with pork instead of dumplings, also a major project, requiring all hands on deck to chop and cook. We could never keep leftovers as there was no place to store them and no refrigerator. If we set any food outside, there were always people, animals, and flies to finish them off for us. So we just kept eating. By the thirteenth month, our food rations ended because we were considered farmers and ate only what we produced.

The sub-brigade leader rang a bell about ten times every morning, signaling us to report to our sub-brigade's designated platform, a concrete slab customarily used for drying grain. We were given ten minutes to assemble. Anyone showing up late would not be given an assignment and, consequently, could not work that day. When we did not work, we did not earn our daily points. We were required—at a bare minimum—to work 325 days a year. Educated youth meeting this minimum requirement for two consecutive years were eligible for selection to work in a non-rural position and to begin receiving rations once again. Some youth would be lucky enough to be allowed to join the army or navy, or even go to college. After reaching the two-year, 325-day threshold, a few fortunate educated youth may even be able to return to Tianjin. You can imagine the motivation we had to attain the minimum points.

Maybe this does not seem so difficult, earning our way off the farm and getting forty days off per year. But it was not that simple. Any bad weather days that prevented us from working were counted as non-workdays. If there was inclement weather for more than forty days, we would not reach our minimums and would therefore be disqualified for relocation out of the rural community. On the one hand, we hoped for bad weather to get a break; on the other hand, we worried about bad weather thwarting our future opportunities.

Work on the farm was always long and backbreaking. A day's assignment might be to clean the pigsty, removing every inch of dung and hauling it in a wheelbarrow to the fertilizer dump, all without gloves, boots, or a mask to diffuse the stench. This job would take a native farmer six to eight hours, but for an inexperienced city dweller like me, it usually took ten to twelve hours. And because the pigsty was cleaned only once a month, the odor was overwhelming. It was one of the worst jobs on the farm.

Another difficult job was harvesting wheat with a sickle, which we would do from sunrise to sunset, typically fourteen to sixteen hours a day. The strands of wheat scratched our skin, the biting insects were constant, and the heat unrelenting. During planting season, we were assigned to plow the fields. We lined up next to the horses and pulled the plow alongside them. Usually there were ten of us to a horse, and the work was so hard, the hunger so great, I remember seeing stars. On one occasion that first summer I fainted.

I weighed 110 pounds and was not strong then. I was working sixteen hours a day from five-thirty in the morning until eleven at night, not eating enough, and depressed about my future. Harvesting wheat was more than my body could withstand. Twice I was transported two miles to a small hospital, where I was given a bed in a room with seven others. I received intravenous fluids, and the doctor told me I

needed rest. He released me the next morning when I was well enough to return to work in the fields.

As hard as cleaning the pigsty and harvesting wheat were, the job I hated the most was creating a crude type of brick used for constructing and repairing buildings by combining clay, straw, and water. Because these substances do not mix well, putting such a concoction into molds along the ground was a grueling task. It required bending over each mold in a contorted, stooped position all day, causing excruciating back pain. I collapsed after only a few hours the first day on the job. As I lay on the ground unable to move, a middle-aged peasant woman, who had been doing such work all her life, commented to me, "It's hard, isn't it? Given time, you'll get used to it." But I tell you, I never did get used to it.

There was always competition for the less taxing jobs on the farm. The job I wanted, but was never "lucky" enough to be assigned, was riding with the horse cart driver to pick up bags of fertilizer from the commune township seat and bring them back to the farm. This meant sitting in the cart for two hours there and two hours back, then hoisting as many fifty-kilo bags of fertilizer that would fit onto the cart—lifting literally tons of this mixture of chemicals and manure—before the cart traveled back to the farm. It was considered a cushy job, usually assigned to an older person, someone's uncle, or someone who enjoyed a favored relationship with the brigade leader.

Our group of thirteen educated youth lived together like a family, though we were split into four different sub-brigades to work during the day. The boy I met on the train, Little Lu, turned out to be a quiet bunkmate. When the day's work was done, he would crawl onto the *kang* to rest until dinner was ready. I distinctly remember his chronic, hacking cough all winter. By then he was smoking the strong tobacco grown on the farm, which seemed to worsen his already poor health.

A girl in our group named Cao was almost the opposite of Little Lu. She was seventeen and tall by Chinese standards, and she loved competing with the "boys." She had a tomboy personality, a ready laugh, and a fiercely competitive spirit. If anyone declared something a "man's job," she would say, "I'm going to do it myself just because you said that!" She had a vibrant personality and was invited to dinner with the party boss's brother. After dining with him, Cao would exclaim, "The dumplings are better there," and let the rest of us split her portion of food. We all loved it when she ate out because it left more food for us. When she was eighteen, Cao legally married the party boss's brother-in-law, Li, and moved into his house, where there was electricity and fewer hardships. We were never sure if she loved him or not, and none of us were invited to the wedding ceremony. To this day, we are still not sure if her parents were even invited, or if they approved of her marriage to a rural resident. Her new husband was a peasant with a darkly weathered complexion and a sixth-grade education. I learned that Cao and her husband later moved to Tianjin, but things did not work out for them. As a peasant, her husband did not qualify for a city job, and his strong country dialect did not help his situation either. There was, and still is, a caste-like system in China, something we in the West might call systematic discrimination against rural residents. Years later I met Cao and the son she had with Li, but she did not want to discuss life at Cheng Village. She told me she was happy working and living in Tianjin with her son.

Two members of our group bonded early on. Ma was a boy who played the violin for us whenever it was raining or storming, or we were not too exhausted from the day's work to enjoy his music. Mozart does not sound so wonderful when you are famished or half asleep. Ma was gregarious and engaging, and early in our time at the farm, the rest of us could see his attraction for the oldest girl in our group, Yun, who had managed to postpone her assignment to the countryside for four years after finishing middle school. Yun had large brown eyes and charming dimples. She looked younger than her age and would routinely tell Ma, "I can't finish all my food, you can have the rest." Ma and Yun were in the same sub-brigade, so he carried her hoe to lighten her load whenever possible.

When Yun became pregnant, it was a serious problem. They wanted to get married and have the baby, but the authorities would not grant them a marriage license. Further, unmarried couples were prohibited access to abortion unless they had a marriage license. Men who caused a pregnancy were subject to severe punishment and even arrest and imprisonment. In a display of bravery, Yun explained to the authorities that she was responsible because she had seduced him. She was ultimately allowed to have an abortion after she and Ma "confessed" and "repented" their mistakes. They both received written reprimands attached to their *dang an*, an official record that follows someone wherever they live. Ma and Yun were in love, and they remained a couple, marrying years later when they returned to the city.

Another woman in our group named Liu, took a quiet and clever approach to being an educated youth. She shared room and board with us in the compound, but rarely had anything to say. After she had worked four weeks in the fields, her father came to visit her, and he made a distinct impression. As the male leader of the group, I greeted him when he paid a visit to the farm, recognizing success in his demeanor and clothing. He wore a Mao uniform that was crisp, not worn-out or thread-bare, and a white shirt. He also wore leather shoes and a watch, two clear signs of status in those days. He had a private conversation with the village party boss and dinner at his house. After he left, Liu was promoted to the position of teacher at Cheng Village school, and after her required two years of service, she was transferred to the county seat, leaving the farm forever.

Many parents of my fellow educated youth visited during the time we were on the farm. They brought the expected gifts and showed their respect for village leaders. After such visits, an educated youth might be assigned an easier job or be shown favoritism in some way. But I did not want my parents to come. The combined train tickets and gifts would have cost them at least 120 *yuan*, which was two months of my father's salary. I regarded it as an unnecessary and impossible expense. Furthermore, I did not care what others on the farm thought of me one way or the other. No matter what I would choose to do, I knew someone would pass judgment. If my parents came, I was seeking favors. If they did not, I was shunning the village. I did not waste time dwelling on it. As a friend remarked later in life: "What others think about you is none of your business."

We have an old saying that officials never criticize those who bring gifts. Everyone knows the intention of a gift is to win favor, an accepted Chinese practice. In fact, being a sycophant is not even frowned upon. There was never any shame in gifting cigarettes to the brigade leader, who, as a result, might ignore your lack of enthusiasm or even assign you fewer or easier tasks for the day. To this day, people gain favor and seek promotion from officials or those in charge by being obsequious, giving gifts, and engaging in other sycophantic behaviors.

Payment for work on the farm was the same no matter what we did. We were paid using a points-earned system instead of money, where points accumulated were of monetary value. A native peasant could earn ten points a day, women eight, and male educated youth workers could earn eight the first year and nine after that. Educated youth, along with all the farmers in the village, would be paid at the Lunar New Year, when all points were summed, and all purchases for food and fuel were deducted from the point total. On the first Lunar New Year, I had only been at the farm for four months. My fellow educated youth and I had not yet learned how to efficiently use the straw as fuel, nor how to cook on a budget. That Lunar New Year of 1975, it was calculated that I owed the brigade nineteen *yuan* because, they said, I had consumed too much fuel and grain. Fortunately, I was allowed to pay my debt out of the next year's points.

The only spending money I had on the farm was the allowance of two *yuan* per month my father provided to buy the things I could not produce myself, such as writing paper, envelopes, stamps, kerosene oil for my lamp, matches, toothpaste, a brush, a towel, and soap. I felt terrible accepting money from my father, when I was the one who should have been earning money to help my parents. Even then I did not spend all he sent me, but saved half, and by the end of the year I had twelve Chinese dollars, a substantial sum of money at the time, to buy a holiday cake for my parents and gifts for my family. All my life I have saved half of everything I have earned. It is a choice, a decision to hold onto something for the future, a habit much like never throwing away food or old clothes, something so deeply ingrained now that I cannot do otherwise. I have always saved to ensure enough money to carry me through the future. It is the only way I can sleep at night.

Our group of educated youth prepared our own meals. Each week that first year, two of us would be assigned to cook for the group, which, to our delight, was our only work assignment for the week. One cook was paid in subsidies, and the second cook was paid in points by the village authority. By our second year on the farm, we were proficient enough that one of us could cook alone, and we rotated the job equally. The week I cooked was a welcome respite from hard labor and the harsh winter cold or the scorching summer heat. In addition, cooking somehow diminished my appetite. Indeed, who has ever heard of a hungry chef? This is when I learned the most about cooking and even began to enjoy it. The person assigned to cooking also guarded our few possessions, as there were no locks, security, or family members to watch over them. The farmers' extended families helped guard their belongings, thus our survival meant functioning as a family as well.

Later the village party boss, Xu, suggested we buy a pig, but none of us knew how to care for one. In Cheng Village, most families raised pigs. The piglets were purchased in early spring, then at the end of the Lunar Year, the pigs were traded for "cash" at the market. Due to our own lack of resources, we were seldom able to feed the poor pig, so it remained skinny. The villagers were amused that our pig was never fat enough to harvest.

At the end of a long day's work, the peasants were occasionally required to go to the four-room village school, where, as educated youth, we would read stories to the poor farmers from a newspaper propagandizing the Communist Party's noble works and such. The reading was slow and boring, the snoring very loud, but this, too, was a requirement. Everyone who worked during the day was required to attend or that day's points would be forfeited. People were never allowed to be idle. Communist Party philosophy aimed to keep everyone physically occupied to minimize the opportunity for counter-revolutionary thinking. This was always their tactic.

Another key strategy of the Communist Party was to eliminate religion so that people would have no other allegiance, certainly not to the influence and power of religion. The government had learned this lesson from other authoritarian countries where religion had been allowed and the people rebelled. That was not about to happen in Mao's China, and religion to this day is still tightly controlled by the government. Only certain religions are recognized as legitimate, and all members are required to register. The gatherings and memberships are still closely watched and regulated.

Because us thirteen educated youth were forced to live together, we did our best to get along. We bonded in our mutual misfortune, empathizing with one another. The boys helped the girls with physically difficult tasks and cooked more frequently in the girls' rooms during winter months to provide warmth. I would not say we were best friends, though some affection emerged within the group.

The relationship between Ma and Yun, though, surprised me. I could not even think about love under our circumstances. By that time in my life, I had garnered a romantic view of love. Chinese fables with descending angels and Shakespeare's *Romeo and Juliet*, the violin concerto of the butterfly and love—these had all influenced me. Indeed "dating" was not allowed anyway. To even spend time together, a couple needed permission from the authorities. An official would check ages and decide whether it was permissible, then tell the couple what they could and could not do. No public displays of affection were acceptable, much less intimacy. To stay in a hotel together a couple needed to produce a marriage license. Mao officially married three times and had many female "assistants," but his government tightly controlled relationships for the entire country. No one questioned the hypocrisy of this double standard.

While I lived on the farm, I did not question why I was there. It never occurred to me. Government propaganda led us to believe that we were better off than 90 percent of the people on earth, and certainly better off than our parents or grandparents. We were indoctrinated to believe that 95 percent of the U.S. population lived in poverty under far worse conditions. Only the elite and exploiting class in the United States enjoyed a good life. We were shown pictures of Black people being beaten, workers being exploited, and police violence. That information and those images kept us going, believing that perhaps we were better off than others.

At the time I lived in the countryside, farmers in China were allotted a piece of land for a house that usually had three rooms and a detached shed. The land also included a small garden to grow vegetables, as well as space for a pig and some chickens. The farmland at large was owned by the government and all the crop yields as well. Life was difficult and insular. Fifteen hundred people lived in the village where I was assigned, but there were only about ten last names. Migrating from one village to another was not allowed, so families—brothers, sisters, grandparents—stayed together. Often the village was named after a family, such as Wang Village or Li Village. If a peasant moved even a few miles away, he would be considered an outsider. And, of course, those in the country were not allowed to move to the city. People lived in one place all their lives, fostering a kind of innocence and naivete about the world at large.

Most of the people in the village were poor by any standard. They certainly had no disposable income. On their small parcel of land, farmers were not given permits to grow any "cash" crop that may bring in extra income during extreme times. Garlic, onions, tobacco, and chili peppers were all strictly monitored because they had a long shelf life and were easy to sell. Farmers were only allowed to grow these crops for personal consumption. The government permitted vegetables like cabbage and eggplant because they would spoil more quickly. Farmers had to accept the reality that if they planted without a permit, village officials would show up with hoes and uproot the whole garden. Brigade leaders shamed those who broke the rules, threatened them, and bullied others not to make the same mistake.

The peasants were, however, allowed to grow small amounts

of tobacco for personal consumption. All the men, and some of the women, smoked homegrown tobacco. A few could afford cigarette papers, but most rolled their dried, homegrown tobacco inside roughly torn pieces of newspaper. These crude cigarettes were narrow on both ends to secure the tobacco and burned so quickly the farmers had to smoke them in seconds or singe their fingers. A few villagers owned special devices for rolling their cigarettes, and a very few could afford to buy premade cigarettes—smooth, white, perfect cylinders that cost two cents each.

Smoking was an important ritual in the village social structure. Brigade leaders all smoked, and those who smoked with them tended to enjoy favored relationships. For one thing, the custom was to share cigarettes, especially with the person in charge, so peasants would give the brigade leader a cigarette to smoke and often another for later, which the leader would tuck on top of his ear, clearly visible to all. Those who curried even more favor would give the leader one to smoke now and two for later, amusingly tucking one on top of each ear!

All the other boys in my group smoked, but I was never able to. It caused severe headaches whenever I tried—and I really did try. My lack of participation in this ritual was suspect. Either I was a wimp who could not even smoke a cigarette, or I was waiting to smoke alone so I would not have to share. In the latter case, I was seen as miserly, and in both cases, I was certainly unintelligent—a cheap wimp. At the time it was believed that smoking helped you to think and make shrewd decisions. Sometimes when I lay down on the ground to rest during a break, the others all jeered that a snake or insects would bite me because I was the only one not protected by tobacco smoke. Although the teasing impelled me to try harder, I still could not make myself into a smoker.

If a peasant was sick or hurt, the only help available within the village tended to be bandages, herbs, aspirin, and basic first aid. In our village, the doctor had been trained by family members. His father had been a doctor, and his father before him. The skills of herbal remedies, acupuncture, and chiropractic were handed down and practiced with reasonable efficiency. The village doctor could also do a modern rabies injection, as well as dispense aspirin. He made house calls, often to the elderly, checking a patient's pulse via touch, examining a patient's tongue, and offering the appropriate remedies.

Serious illnesses, however, required a trip to the township's ten-bed hospital, where a Western-style trained doctor had access to more sophisticated tools such as an x-ray machine or intravenous equipment. The township doctor was the only one who wore a mask, which was also considered advanced medical equipment at the time because only medical personnel wore them. Surgery was not available except at the hospital forty kilometers away in the county seat, which had a population of 800,000, comprised of twenty-five towns. If the situation was serious, the brigade leader would send a horse and cart to carry a patient that distance. Otherwise family members would have to haul the sick individual to the hospital in a large wheelbarrow or on the back of a bicycle.

No peasant owned a horse or cow to pull a cart, and the use of these animals was strictly controlled by the brigade leader.

Few people even owned a bicycle. The only vehicle I remember seeing while on the farm was the army jeep provided for the head of the county government. Transportation was seldom necessary when there was no place to go.

As the male group leader, I would go with my female counterpart regularly to meet with the accountant and assess our group's finances. These meetings took place in the evening when the accountant's wife was home to bring us extra hot water for tea. She was a particularly kind woman who worked in my sub-brigade during the day and helped me when she could. I came to know her well, along with the village doctor, since I got sick quite often. On several occasions, the village doctor invited me into his house to sleep on the end of their *kang* to sweat out my fevers. Overall, I have fond memories of the many kind villagers.

It was a welcome distraction when every two to three months, weather permitting, a traveling open-air cinema team would arrive to show a movie. They would string a white sheet between trees to use as the screen, and the peasants would gather on one of the four sub-brigade concrete areas. The entire village came to watch the movie, and sometimes even those from nearby villages would walk miles across farmland to be entertained. I remember a sense of civility and joy surrounding these events, for it was all the entertainment we knew at the time.

We saw a total of only eight different movies, every one of them centered around revolutionary themes, featuring Peking opera performers or dancers from the Shanghai ballet. Even the most refined actors and dancers wore military-type clothing to dramatize Mao's propaganda. The Female Detachment of the Red Army showed beautiful women in pointe shoes leveling guns and slashing swords as they did their dainty leg kicks and pirouettes. It was an amazing sight. The farmers loved it, and they loved going out to take a pause from their difficult lives to watch these pretty women standing on their pointe shoes with rifles in hand—aimed right at them! The absurdity of the situation was part of the entertainment.

Another movie told the story of "The White-Haired Woman," a fable familiar to most Chinese at that time. In this operatic film, a farmer who is unable to pay his rent to the landowner is asked to relinquish his daughter as payment. Unable to comply with such a request, the father commits suicide, and his daughter runs away into the woods never to be seen again. Years later a white-haired woman is spotted in the same woods, and when food is left out for her, it disappears. Is she the daughter's ghost or someone else? The answer glorified the Communist government: the old society of landlords was evil, just as the Japanese were evil, and the whole world outside of China was plotting to destroy us. When Mao's army arrived, the white-haired girl came out of the woods and married her childhood lover, a commanding officer in the army who had liberated her hometown. The message was clear—only Mao could save anyone.

The ballet dancers in army uniforms with short pants, pointed shoes, and guns implied what we were repeatedly told—that we would only win the revolution with two barrels, the barrel of the gun and the barrel of the pen. That was how the

Communist Party won the war, and that is how they have retained control. The lesson of gun and pen was one of the quotes found in Mao's *Little Red Book*. The victory of the revolution depended upon those two barrels, and this was reinforced by the hierarchy of the government departments, with the army at the top, followed closely by the Department of Propaganda.

Like all educated youth, I was given Mao's *Little Red Book* when I was in elementary school. It took a few years for the government to print and distribute enough books to ensure that each of the 700,000,000 Chinese citizens at that time owned a copy. We were required to keep the book with us at all times and to hold it high during any public gatherings, as Mao's second in command, Lin Piao, demonstrated whenever he was standing or sitting next to Mao. Lin was largely instrumental in publishing Mao's teachings in a book, with his name credited on the back of the front cover. Lin Piao, a successful and intelligent general, was at one time Mao's designated successor, but over time Mao felt threatened by Lin's increasing popularity and decided he wanted him out. Fearing for his life, Lin boarded an airplane to Russia where he planned to defect, but the plane mysteriously crashed over Mongolia, killing him and the family members who were with him. It was another unexplained incident that occurred during the Mao regime.

When I was in fifth and sixth grade, Mao's *Little Red Book* was my only textbook. We memorized, recited, and discussed the quotations. I learned at an early age that Mao's quotations held the answer to any question and could be relied upon to help us overcome any obstacle. If a deaf person read Mao's book, he would then hear. A mute person would be able to speak clearly after reading Mao's book. That is what we were taught.

> *Politics is war without blood and war is politics with blood. Communism is not love; it is a hammer to crush the enemy.*

These are examples of the quotes, poems, and lessons contained in the children's version of the *Little Red Book: The Greatest Instruction*. Quotations contained in the adult version tended to be more elaborate, such as this classic quote from Mao in 1927:

> *Revolution is not a dinner party nor writing an essay nor painting a picture nor doing embroidery. It cannot be so refined and leisurely, so temperate, kind, courteous, and restrained and magnanimous.*
>
> *What is revolution?*
>
> *It is an insurrection, an act of violence by which one class overthrows another.*

Despite all the obvious propaganda that Mao's China was better than the old China, the villagers loved the highly entertaining movies and always looked forward to movie night. I remember climbing a tree like other young people to get a better view. It was a rare time when we all relaxed together and had fun.

CHAPTER IV

My Education
Tianjin

1956 – 1976

The Chinese calendar, which can be traced back to the fourteenth century B.C.E., follows the lunar cycle, and is still used by both rural and urban residents to gauge the week or month. The fifteenth day of each lunar month coincides with the full moon, as do major holidays such as Moon Festival, Lunar New Year, and the Lantern Festival. Dragon Raise His Head Day falls on the second day of the second lunar month, marking the end of the new year holiday festivities when farmers return to work and resume planting.

Those of us from the city were allowed to return home to visit our families for ten to fourteen days during the Lunar New Year. As the youth group leader that first year, I could not leave until another member of our group returned to the farm, so someone was there to guard our belongings. I had been in the countryside for six months and traveled back to Tianjin in a state of despair. As the eldest and only son, I had always believed I needed to be the protector and provider to my family. But I was returning home to them a burden. The shame I felt was unbearable.

I was born in 1956, my parents' seventh child, but the first to survive. My mother took herbal medicine daily for one hundred days prior to my birth, boiling herbs into a broth or tea to drink every day. After I was born, my parents visited the Buddhist temple for spiritual guidance on who I was and how I could best survive. A Buddhist monk advised my parents on the elements I possessed and those I lacked. In Chinese culture, there are five elements: gold, wood, water, fire, and earth. I was born lacking gold and any other metal, as well as water—and so was given a name that provided those two elements. *Tie* (pronounced 'tea') is iron or steel, and it means strength. *Han* has a water component and implies a strong person. As is customary in China, my parents and others repeated my name over and over, almost like a chant, to reinforce its meaning. The more a person hears his or her name, the more the meaning of the name influences and endures. My Chinese friends have always called me *Tiehan,* the "Iron Man."

It was tradition to give all children in a family the same first name as the first-born child. As such, all three of my sisters' names start with *Tie*. My oldest sister, *Tieying*, was born two years after me, *Tierong* two years after that, and *Tiewei*, another three years later. When my mother was pregnant, the family did not allow her to carry water or anything heavy, and when the baby was born, we kept the window closed, believing the outside air would cause disease in later years. Tradition in China dictated different kinds of responsibilities for boys, so I was too busy to get to know my sisters well when we were growing up. As adults we became very close. My family had a gentle energy. Through our thin apartment walls, we could hear other households in heated disputes, but we were not like that. My father's education and my mother's kindness rose above our difficult circumstances.

I attended the neighborhood school six days a week, using textbooks and notebooks to do my homework. Because we were poor and notebooks and pencils were a luxury, kids in my neighborhood used chalk on the narrow concrete street outside our houses to practice math problems and write words. We purchased four pieces of chalk for just one *fen*, which was much cheaper than buying pencils at three *fen* each. Whenever the weather permitted, I remember going out right after school to chalk off a square, reserving space to do my homework. I memorized Chinese characters, poems, multiplication tables, and later, the chemical elements chart and physics equations.

I started out and remained a diligent student and a dutiful son. Many of the sixty children in my elementary school class, both girls and boys, did not pay attention in class. Their eyes roamed around, they talked while the teacher was explaining, and they did not do their homework. I had learned from my father to stand up when the teacher came to my desk and to take my homework seriously. The praise I received from the teachers earned me respect, but my poverty was obvious. My clothes were heavily patched, and my shoes so worn that sometimes my toes would poke out of the holes. Everyone in class distinguished the families who had little from those who had nice shoes and a family bicycle. Our family was often ridiculed and marginalized even outside the classroom.

In the sixties and seventies when I grew up, the possessions that most demonstrated success in life were a bicycle, a watch, and a sewing machine, because they all turned. But a radio was the real jackpot. We called these prized items three turns and one sound. Attractive women sought to marry rich men who could provide such "luxuries." Officials who worked for the Communist Party made more money and were often regaled with gifts, which was obvious to children as well as their parents. In my class, however, not a single student came from a family that owned a telephone. Only high-ranking government officials were permitted to use them.

Somehow meritocracy survived this class system. Starting in kindergarten, our performance and test scores were published on big character posters, ranked by name for everyone to see. At the end of the year, parents of the top three students were asked to stand up in a recognition ceremony held during the annual parent-teacher conference in our home classroom with all sixty parents. No students were present because the room was not large enough to hold everyone.

Every year I was among the top three achievers in my class, and one of my parents (only one parent per child was allowed to attend) had the honor of standing before other parents, who would then learn that their son was smart. It is difficult to overstate the social impact of this kind of recognition. Some parents would beat their children in public for being at the bottom of the class ranking and some students were required to attend summer school to catch up. All such consequences were considered shameful.

As a top student, I also enjoyed material rewards for superior performance. I received a pencil with an eraser that would have cost me five *fen*. Only the very privileged owned a pencil like that. When it got too small to hold, I attached a little pencil hat to extend its length and when it became too short to sharpen, I would take out what was left of the lead and poke it into a mechanical pencil. Not one scrap was wasted.

Sometimes I was bullied by two or three boys who resented their parents for using me as an exemplary son: "Look at him he is such a good student," "He helps his mother cook, he takes out the night pot," "Why can't you be more like Tiehan?" and so on. In our neighborhood, we all knew what went on. We could hear when families were fighting or when a child was being beaten for failing to be a good student. School mattered.

There were no late bloomers. If students fell behind academically, they would be required to attend summer school. If they failed three out of five subjects in summer school, they would have to repeat the entire grade, and if it happened again, they would repeat until too old to continue. In China at that time, compulsory education ended at ninth grade for urban students and sixth grade for rural students. When students could not progress beyond middle school, they were finished. For me, school was a way of making my parents proud and feeling good about myself. I worked hard and always did well.

But the Cultural Revolution turned the education system upside down. In Tianjin, all schools shut down from 1966 to 1968. Because they were educated, teachers were automatically suspected counterrevolutionaries. Some teachers, including professors at universities, were even sent off to work on farms, while kids loitered on the streets during the day, running loose, being on the lookout for the next thing the Red Guard chose to ravage in the city. From 1966 to 1968, the Red Guard took down everything they considered "old world." Mao told the Red Guards to break the "old world" into pieces, which included anything feudal, capitalistic, or imperial. Photos, vases, paintings, frames, furniture, books, nearly all people's possessions were destroyed. Kids hung out waiting to see what would happen next. The Red Guards requested that people with "old stuff" voluntarily bring them to the street intersections to be destroyed in public via smashing or fire. If the Red Guards came to your house and discovered such old things, they would continue their rampage, smashing even more items. I recall my maternal grandmother having to take a pair of antique porcelain vases to an intersection in Tianjin, where she watched them shatter into pieces against the concrete ground.

Students were allowed to return to elementary school in 1968, but we learned little more than Mao's sayings. At the time students were encouraged to treat teachers disrespectfully, yelling and throwing things at them during class. Teachers had no incentive to instruct as they had before the shutdown.

In 1970 I moved on to middle school. Tianjin is a premiere northern port city, and during the Qing Dynasty, parts of the city were granted to foreign countries as "concessions" for unequal treaties that allowed these countries trade access within China. Each country's parcel of land was designed to reflect its architecture, religions, trade, food, and customs. If you went to French Town, it would feel as though you were in France, on a "rue" with a towering cathedral. Starting in the late 1800s, concessions emerged for Italy, France,

Belgium, Austria-Hungary, Great Britain, Japan, Russia, and Germany. To this day those structures and areas exist in Tianjin, although their former residents are long gone. Mao drove them all out in 1949.

The people of Tianjin continued to use the buildings after the original inhabitants had been expelled. The middle school I entered in 1970, the New Study Academy or *Xin Xue*, occupied a former Catholic school and convent inside the British concession. The church, stripped of crosses and religious symbols, was the auditorium, the pews removed, to allow a full grade of 500 to 550 students to sit on the floor at one time. The first time I entered that church, I thought, "This doesn't look like China." The shadow on the wall where the cross once hung was still visible, and it inspired me to gravitate toward something different, something larger and more powerful. I loved being in that former church with its soaring domed ceiling, chandeliers, and balconies along the side walls and wooden floors. I had never walked on wooden floors before then and discovered how different shoes sound on wood than they do on concrete or dirt. I was in awe of that magnificent place.

Four different elementary schools fed into my middle school, with more than 1,500 students divided into eight classes. Because I was a good student, I became part of the school's propaganda department, a select group of students who produced a paper every other day about common heroes, like a boy who kept marching despite blisters on his feet. We looked for good news in the Mao tradition. This is where I met one of my best friends, Kai Dong, a kind and good student with excellent handwriting. He was proficient at using a manual mimeograph "copying machine," consisting of a metal sheet and carbon. Paper was pulled over the screen and, using a roller brush, he would print copies.

Because Kai Dong's father worked as a low-level government official, they were more well-to-do by our standards at the time. They lived in a one-and-a-half-room apartment and owned a bicycle. They did not experience hunger as my family did, but they were generous people. Our mothers had met and liked each other instantly, and the two families became friends. Kai Dong knew how to cut hair, and in high school he gave free haircuts to the teachers and principal. He was very well liked. In those days, a wash and cut cost twenty-five cents. Even hooligans in class were nice to Kai Dong, hoping to get a free haircut. He had a reputation for being such a generous person and a good barber that, upon graduation from high school, he was able to choose his job. He joined the public security bureau, which inspects suspicious mail, working in a prestigious office. Later he received an all-expense paid scholarship to college for two years. We are friends to this day.

Sunhui from middle school became another lifelong friend. He, too, worked in the propaganda department and later became a truck driver. Everyone in the propaganda department was a good student and had different responsibilities. I did much of the newspaper writing, Kai Dong used his calligraphy skills and ran the printer, and Sunhui, who was tall and strong, was charged with equipment repair and maintenance. The girls in the group used their lovely voices to make announcements and did readings from several government newspapers over the school's public address system.

Middle school friends

Middle school was not always joyful. Mao had ordered three groups to jointly run each school. At the top was the Working Class Mao's Thoughts Propaganda Detachment. To be in this leadership contingent, one could have no more than an elementary education, though no education at all was preferable. Everything about education was upside down in those days. The middle group in the school hierarchy was the military, usually a lieutenant and two privates. The principal and teachers were at the bottom. These three groups made joint decisions about the curriculum and rules of the school.

Every morning before class we would run and goose-step around the grounds. We were equipped with rifles and learned to shoot. This military training was to prepare us for war—most likely with the Soviet Union. To this end we went camping, as it was called, for two weeks during the winter holiday of my eighth and ninth grade years. Because it was very cold, we were allowed to bring quilts, but other than that, we had no camping equipment or gear. We marched twenty to thirty miles a day to the countryside, staying with farmers—three or four students per farmer—who were not happy to have us there, sleeping in their houses and eating their food. We were not equipped with footwear appropriate for marching so many miles. Most of us wore the cloth shoes our mothers made, and by the end of the day, we would have severe blisters. We would gather around a basin of hot water, sometimes eight of us to one basin, where we would pop and rinse the blisters to be ready to march again the next day. We feared walking too slowly or getting sick lest we be ostracized for not being brave or "Red" enough.

During our daily marches, the leaders purposely waited until we were in the most awkward places, like the peak of a hill or in the eye of the storm, then ordered us to eat our lunches. Furthermore, we were not allowed to complain, and were often reminded how the revolutionary martyrs died for us.

When we were not marching to the countryside, we were still marching every day at school. Classes were regularly interrupted by military-style training. An adult announced through the loudspeaker when it was time to "gather on the playground," and instantly the entire school of 1,500 students would mobilize. Each of us had a number, a group, an assigned route to exit the building, and a specific place to stand on the playground. We had only sixty seconds to get to our position on the playground. To achieve this record time, we were subjected to hours and hours of training. When we were all gathered, we would stand at military attention before being granted permission to sit on the ground listening to speeches and receiving Mao's latest instructions. Some days we would be forced to endure up to several hours of lectures from Working Propaganda Department officials about how depraved and inhumane the former Nationalist government was, and how much better we lived without the exploitation of the bourgeois capitalists. It was brutal—there was no shade, no shelter, and no breaks. Some students wet their pants.

In middle school, "bitter tasting events" forced all students to experience firsthand the horrors of what people ate before the Communists took over. A nosh was prepared using the dregs of tofu, tea leaves, corn flour, and other scraps like shredded grass. We had been so brainwashed that we ate it and said it was good. We believed we were supposed to say that. Objecting, the workers in the school replied, "No, it is not good food." What did we know? Reality was irrelevant under Mao. Many people were willing to die for him, and we all learned to say whatever the government wanted to hear. We were afraid of being labeled counterrevolutionaries and did or said anything necessary to avoid the wrath of the government.

After two years, the government seemed to realize that involving workers and the military in school administration was dysfunctional, served no real purpose, and was even counterproductive. Deng Xiaoping, who had been instrumental in China's economic reconstruction after the 1959-61 famine, was expelled from the government in 1966. When he returned to power in 1972, workers returned to the factories, soldiers returned to the military, and students began learning again. Deng did not last long, however. Mao appointed him vice premiere in 1974, then expelled him again in 1976.

While in middle school I met Mr. Wu, who was to be a profound influence in my life. He taught middle school English in a different part of Tianjin, and my father had met him through a mutual acquaintance. One day when my father and I were shopping for food at the market, we ran into Mr. Wu, and I helped him carry vegetables and coal home—it was a heavy load, and he was not a hardy man. He asked me in conversation if I enjoyed learning English in school, and when I replied that I loved it, he offered to tutor me every Sunday evening. My father advised that if he were me, he would accept the opportunity, and of course, I was delighted. A few other students from different schools joined our study session and we used our government-issued textbook, the only one we had. Mr. Wu had saved some textbooks during his years in Great Britain and the United States, and although they had no Chinese translations, we used them as well.

When a representative of the Neighborhood Committee found out what we were doing, she reported us to the authorities. Informing on neighbors and friends was common and encouraged in China then, as it is to this day. We were all summoned to the police department to be questioned about our anti-government activity. We denied the allegations, showing the police our China-published English textbook, saying we are only learning that communism is better than capitalism, learning Mao's slogans, and how to say, "Don't move or I shall shoot." The police did not understand English, so they did not realize that Mr. Wu was calling them "bloody bastards" to their faces. We were left to our learning after that.

Paying Mr. Wu for "unauthorized" English lessons would have put him and my parents at additional risk of punishment. Nevertheless, we were eager to show our gratitude somehow, so my mother made him dumplings in her kind and generous way, using our ration of pork and wheat flour. Through my English language sessions, I developed a close and enduring friendship with Mr. Wu.

In the winter of 1976, when I returned to Tianjin, feeling desperate and facing a bleak future, I decided to pay a visit to Mr. Wu. I trusted him and sensed that he would understand. I expressed to him how bad it was for me, how I was a burden to my family, that life was physically and mentally unbearable, and how useless I felt to my parents. They cannot be proud of me, I told him, because I have no power, no connections, and no income.

It was then he confided his story to me. As a young man he had been educated in Great Britain and the United States and spoke beautiful British English. When the Communists asked Chinese emigres to return to their mother country to help build the new China, he believed in them. He gave up his life in the West, and he and his well-educated wife went back to Beijing where he became one of the first group of announcers for Radio Peking.

Eventually his intelligence and capability became a threat to the Communist Party, and he was moved to a lower-profile position in the ministry of foreign trade, working with state-owned import and export corporations. In 1957, he was labeled a Rightist, an enemy of the people, and demoted to teaching middle-school English in Tianjin, a move that signaled he was no longer important, not trusted, incapable. He had been promised a glorious future, but there he was, living as a nearly impoverished middle school teacher with almost nothing.

He empathized with me in my despair, and after patiently listening to me, he said kindly, "I'll help you learn English." He handed me a textbook, a notebook, and postage stamps, telling me to mail my homework to him monthly, then he would mail it back with corrections. He also suggested I listen to the radio, where English was taught three times a day. This was in 1976, after Nixon had been to China, and George Bush Sr. was the U.S. ambassador living in Beijing; there was interest then in connecting with the English-speaking world. However, we had no radios on the farm, only a loudspeaker for announcements. After I explained to my father what Mr. Wu told me, he said nothing; he was never a big talker, but he was a great listener. In his quiet way, he did good deeds without saying much or expecting anything back. The day I was to return to the farm, my father gifted me a turquoise blue transistor radio that cost him half a month's salary. I still have the radio to this day! My father had such faith in me, I vowed to myself to do my best. I gained much strength and confidence from my parents. Their intense, unfailing support and belief in me was my good fortune.

CHAPTER V

HOPE
CHENG VILLAGE

1976 – 1978

I proudly took the battery-operated radio back to the village and began to seriously study English, memorizing words, spellings, and tenses, and navigating all the irregularities of the language. A hole was what we dug; a hoe was the tool we used to dig. Everyone in the village thought I was a lunatic, reciting these things as I worked in the fields. "You're repairing the surface of the earth," they said. "You don't need English. Are you going to speak English to a cow?"

I always loved learning English starting at an early age. In middle school, our teacher tried to teach, but she never attended high school, and having received only twelve months of English training, her pronunciation was terrible. But hardly anyone cared. The idea of learning English was so far-fetched at the time that failing the class was inconsequential. We only learned propaganda slogans anyway, like "Down With The U.S. Imperialists." Because I loved it and worked hard to learn, I always placed first in English out of my grade of 500 students.

But my pace of learning accelerated once I began working with Mr. Wu. There is a Chinese saying: "The load of skills has never broken anyone's back." Despite the ongoing Cultural Revolution, during which many intellectuals were punished both mentally and physically for knowing a foreign language, my father and Mr. Wu had encouraged me to learn English when I was in high school. Perhaps it was blind faith that kept me going. Indeed, those Sunday afternoons changed my life.

But learning English in school did not mean we were taught anything positive about American culture. Mao only favored movements, revolutions, and events that reflected U.S. culture in negative ways. He would delight in exploiting and spreading misinformation about U.S. social and political strife to his advantage. In China, we did not hear Western news or music on the radio. In fact, people could go to jail for listening to enemy stations from the United States, Taiwan, or Japan. On my radio at the farm, I listened only to Radio Beijing, which was authorized to teach English via Mao's slogans and the military language of the Communist Party. Notwithstanding the subject matter, it turned out to be an invaluable tool for learning English.

In summer on the farm, we worked until ten p.m., and I would miss the English lessons being taught on the radio. To my good fortune, they were repeated three different times during the day, and being committed and determined, I tuned in whenever I had the opportunity. I would not learn until later the major impact that this studying was to have on my life. At the time, I could not imagine where it would lead me, but I felt I was moving forward in some way. I had a sense of responsibility and felt more "useful" now that I had a radio, lessons, and the faith and support of both my father and Mr. Wu. I had my high school textbooks with me and studied to memorize as much as I could about physics and history, and anything that engaged my mind. Learning opened new possibilities and gave me purpose and hope. Truly, it saved me. Then the politics of education in China took another turn, and my life changed again with one critical announcement on the village loudspeaker.

The compound for educated youths included an office with a public address system for announcements, but more urgent messages were transmitted via a loudspeaker set up in the center of the village where we dried the grain. This loudspeaker was thirty feet high and could be heard by all 1,500 villagers. I hated the loud blaring of the mostly mundane announcements. The news was read to us at eight every evening, and it was in this way on September 9, 1976, we learned that Mao had died. We did not know he was sick, for how could he possibly have a disease like ordinary people? After all, we were constantly wishing him ten thousand years of life!

In our minds, Mao was larger than life, taller than most Chinese men, and infallible. He could orate for an hour without notes and knew everything about Chinese history. We had not expected his death, nor would anyone ever speculate about it, for that would have been a dangerous betrayal. It was a total shock, but I clearly remember feeling happy. No leader could cause more suffering than he had—his replacement could not be worse.

The cause of Mao's death at age eighty-three is still unknown, and he was never buried or cremated. He remains, to this day, in a clear shrine in Tiananmen Square where, for a fee, anyone can view his preserved body through the glass case. At the time of his death, every village was expected to hold a vigil in his honor. Some people cried uncontrollably, chanting "Long live Mao" and "Ten thousand years of Mao." He was already dead, and they still thought he would live forever. At that time, many in China relied only on Mao and his dictates, hanging on his every word. When he died, they were lost. I remember seeing the expressions on the farmers' faces. Everything they did was based on Mao's policy. Hence, when the source of their instruction was gone, what would happen to them? I sensed their anxiety and deep concern.

One immediate benefit of Mao's death was being allowed to listen to Peking Opera again. But even better news was to come. Just over one year after his death, on October 25, 1977, I heard over the loudspeaker what I had been waiting years to hear: China would now resume the national college entrance exam system which had been suspended in 1966 at the start of the Cultural Revolution. For ten years, the government had ceased the academic exam that allowed passing students to register for college. Technically colleges had reopened in 1970, but only to select students based on the whims of Communist Party officials. There was no test, and bribes were not uncommon. Often students who were chosen opted to study philosophy or Marxism and graduated to become party officials. And during those years, college was reduced to a three-year program.

Poor people and those not connected to the government, meaning those lacking the powerful networks of *guanxi*, had absolutely no chance of going to college during those years.

After Mao's death, political skirmishes among party leaders followed before Deng Xiaoping returned to a high post in July 1977. Unlike Mao and his closest allies, Deng believed in learning and personal development. He himself had been educated in France. As such, he quickly moved to reinstate the National College Entrance Exam, the *gaokao*.

The night I heard the announcement, I could not sleep. I somehow knew I would do well on the test, and that this was my way out. The next morning, I went to the commune seat to inform the leader of Educated Youth Office, Mr. Wang, that I wanted to register for the exam. He did not know what I was talking about. What exam? They had not received any official documentation yet. After nearly two months of bureaucracy, our village government officials finally received confirmation of this news.

Xu Jiao Hua, the village leader, was a memorable character in my destiny. He was tall—over six feet—and had come to the village specifically to be its leader. His father, a government official, would occasionally visit, arriving in a chauffeur-driven Jeep, speaking excellent Mandarin, demonstrating confidence and power. Xu's father's Mao uniform was made of fine fabric that was obviously not hand washed in a creek. This man's son, our village leader, also called the Party secretary, had the power to determine the fate of each person in our village. He approved who left the village, who was assigned to the army, and who could take the college exam. He was, in fact, the government. But I never found him to be abusive or corrupt.

Everyone in the village thought I was crazy, deluded, foolish. The lunatic with his English verbs now wanted to take a college test! Registration for this test was highly regulated, another way the government controlled who would or would not be educated. First, a person had to be politically "reliable," as China was not about to educate anyone who would betray Communist Party principles. Those registering needed to be certified that they had worked 325 days a year for two years. Applicants could not be handicapped or have a communicable disease, and no time off was allowed for test preparation. This was to protect us from the consequences of failing the test and missing our annual required days of work. Or so I was told.

The Cheng Village Party Committee certified that I was a qualified applicant, granting me the official "signature" of the red chop. Local officials did not sign their names to documents, but endorsed all official papers using the red chop, which our village leader kept safely locked inside his desk drawer. I took and passed the required physical examination, and Mr. Wu sent books to help me prepare for the college entrance exam. I knew how to study; it came naturally to me.

Years earlier, just as I was finishing middle school, high school had resumed in China. We stayed in the same building as in middle school, but the rooms were better, and in that setting it was admirable to pursue academic excellence. Learning was commended and I quickly rose to the top of my class. I loved learning, though many in high school did not. To them high school was a temporary way to avoid being sent to the farm, the lesser of two evils in their eyes.

For me it was so much more. I can say that I was happy in high school, especially when the government did not interfere. My name went on the posters commending high-performing students. I enjoyed rigorous teaching and learning real things. I did actual problem solving, calculated algebraic equations, studied Newton's force and counterforce, how steam moved things, facts that I welcomed and loved knowing. I embraced the challenge of school, and for almost two years learning was not only "allowed," it was encouraged.

After those two good years of high school, the country's thinking shifted again. Things were always changing. Suddenly this campaign to educate was wrong. Deng had been the champion for broad education, but when he was purged, teachers were ridiculed and even punished for being good. The best math teacher would be demoted to an assistant, and an inept person would take over. Nothing ever made sense. Good students were targeted, too, and I was one of them. I was designated as "works too hard on academics." Mostly it was verbal shaming, part of the Rightest Revisionist campaign against those who advocated education that did not focus solely on Mao's quotes and philosophy.

We continued to participate in military marches in high school, but less frequently and only on weekends. In spite of the drills, I was happy to be learning, happy to be there. I made good friends in high school, many were also my friends in middle school, and we remain friends today. I was appointed head of the student council, another reason I knew so many students in the school. I was honored and enjoyed the privileges of being president of the Student Group in high school and being a leader in my middle school Propaganda Department, learning organizational and leadership skills from both positions. From the time I was very young, I seemed to have a talent for managing peer relationships. I believe I inherited this trait from my extroverted mother.

High school ended without fanfare. There was no ceremony and no diploma other than a group document stating the year of graduation and the names of the graduates. The old formalities about school and graduation were considered bourgeois. In fact, we were taught that everything old was rubbish. Furthermore, whether we studied and learned or did nothing for the two years of high school, we still graduated. Job salaries were the same for middle school graduates and high school graduates. We were the first high school graduation class in Tianjin during the Cultural Revolution. Those brief but happy years awakened my desire for learning.

All those memories came flooding back as I studied for the college exam. Near the end of December 1977, I reported to the township high school for three days of testing in math, Chinese, history, geography, and political science. There was never any "science," only party doctrine and slogans. The language part of the test was optional that first year, but I eagerly walked eighteen miles to the county seat to take it. The written English test went as expected, but the oral part of the exam lasted all of five minutes. The tester was not exactly an expert in oral English. "You pass," she said and let it go at that. She had no idea if I was speaking correctly or not.

Then I waited. I had a sense that I had done well, though

the math section had been a challenge. We were told that 5,700,000 people took the test that year. Examinees' ages ranged from eighteen to twenty-eight-year-olds who had waited ten years to take the exam. I knew that I was up against fierce competition. The test was scored on a curve and a rigid cutoff established with no exceptions. There was no acceptance committee looking at other achievements or calculating anything other than the numerical test score. We did not know how many students the government would accept, but we assumed it would be a limited number because college was free. College students were not permitted to work. Once you entered college, it was your entire focus. Despite the fierce competition, I was cautiously optimistic. I had a good feeling.

When the Lunar New Year arrived, the village leader said to me, "Go home and wait for the good news." I often think back to that statement. Even in our harsh village life, this man seemed to know I would be able to move on. He was the one who had given me the red chop affirming my good character, and his tone was encouraging. I went home and continued to wait with anticipation. In a calming way, my mother assured me that all would be fine either way; she didn't want me to feel any pressure. My father remained silent as always.

College acceptance announcements were sent as telegrams in large nine-by-twelve-inch envelopes, with dark brown calligraphy on the front, delivered by a mailman riding a motorcycle. Telegrams, good or bad, always carried urgent news. Right before the Lunar New Year of 1978, the motorcycle arrived in my neighborhood—loud, imposing, and as out of place as a dragon. A crowd gathered to see what was happening. When they realized that it was my college acceptance letter, they were euphoric. In our neighborhood, the highest-level job anyone might attain was bus driver or machine operator. Nobody went to college. College meant leaving the working class to become an intellectual. It meant being automatically propelled into an elite socioeconomic class.

The Cultural Revolution had turned everything upside down, and people were often rude to one another because they were impoverished and downtrodden. But on that day, I earned approval from the elders and admiration from my peers. The little kids jumped in excitement, and my parents stood watching proudly. There was an air of exhilaration, a sense of hope and pride that these people rarely had the opportunity to experience. In that backward, dilapidated neighborhood, something so good had emerged, like a phoenix rising. Something happened that was not supposed to happen. The motorcycle driver told us it was the only acceptance letter he had ever delivered in our neighborhood of more than 100,000 people. "I want to see this fellow," he said.

I was speechless. I did not care where I would be attending college. It didn't matter. This one event, this acceptance letter, would change my life. I knew that as well as everyone there. I would be issued an official college badge and would wear it proudly every day for the next four years. When I went into shops or got onto the bus, I would be treated with respect. It is difficult to overstate the extent to which attending college elevated one's status in China at that time.

For the next few days, neighbors dropped off small gifts and stopped by to wish me well. A good high school friend, Chun-Sheng, visited me before I left. He, too, had taken the exam, but he did not receive enough points to pass. Seeing his disappointment, I offered him my turquoise transistor radio to help him learn English. Chung-Sheng and I remained friends, and thirty years later, when I was in Tianjin, we got together and he returned the radio, which had helped him as it had helped me. "You keep it now," he told me. It was a very emotional moment.

My friend Sunhui got permission to use a truck to drive me to the farm and back so I could pick up my few possessions. While riding with him to the village, I noticed how the dirt and dust stayed behind us in a motorized vehicle. This was very different from being in horse-drawn carts, where the rider was always surrounded by a cloud of dust. We gathered up my belongings and packed them inside the cab of the truck with us. We did not even need to use the back bed, my possessions were so few.

I was the second of the thirteen educated youth to leave Cheng Village, but eventually everyone left. In late 1978, youth assigned to the countryside rebelled, protesting with signs that said, "We Want To Go Home," and "Let Me Go Home Or I'll Die." In one blatant and risky move, 300 young people laid down on the train tracks to show they would rather die than take the train to the countryside. They were not sure if the train would stop for them, because in China at that time, human life was dispensable. If an authority figure told you to stop or he would shoot, the odds were he would follow through on the threat. But in the case of the 300 who rebelled, the train stopped and their lives were spared. It was the beginning of the end of Mao's program to reeducate youths in the countryside.

As harsh as it was, my own situation could have been much worse. Many educated youths were sent, not to farms, but to military-type installations along critical borders with Burma, Mongolia, Siberia, and Tibet. Thousands would be sent to one location, provided meals, uniforms, and militia training. At one time, I had actually considered joining the military training camp at the Mongolian border. Had I chosen that path, I would have never learned English or taken the entrance exam. Military leaders in such camps followed nothing other than their own agendas. Going to a military camp would have completely altered the trajectory of my life,

As I prepared to leave the farm, I had mixed feelings about leaving the people I had lived with in the village. We were all sad. Indeed, it was not fair that they were forced to remain in the life we all wanted to escape. It was a difficult goodbye, and I knew I would miss them. I was leaving people with whom I developed deep relationships. If I was ever offered another chance to relocate to the countryside, I would choose not to go. As I have often said, misfortune can be the best school, if you get to graduate from it. Unfortunately, many of the educated youth did not graduate from their misfortune. The village leader confided that he was sure I would be admitted to college and, to celebrate, invited me to dine on dumplings at his home. I think they all realized that by "being a lunatic" and learning all that English grammar, I had found my way out. It is possible that all of us shared a sense that maybe things were changing, that maybe there was hope.

As part of the application process, I was required to submit the names of five colleges where I would like to study, then admissions staff would review the applicants and make their choices. As a pious son, I selected colleges that were all in the north, in Tianjin or near Beijing, to be near my parents. Instead I was placed at Changsha Railway College in the capital of Hunan province, 1,200 miles south of Tianjin. At the time, each ministry in China ran its own college to prepare students to fill jobs the ministry needed. Thus, the aviation, mining, and railroad ministries all administered their own colleges. The Changsha Railway College mostly prepared engineers to build locomotives and railway cars, but they also had a foreign languages department, which is where I was placed. My strong performance on the English portion of the entrance exam might have been the deciding factor that secured my acceptance into college.

Learning foreign language skills was not encouraged in those days. For many years under Mao, you could be dragged into the street and beaten for speaking English—or for wearing fancy leather shoes or doing anything that appeared bourgeois. Anyone who spoke English would pretend they did not. Russian was the only language allowed under Mao, until Nikita Khrushchev came into power, after which studying Russian became unpopular as well.

For me, learning English opened the door to a whole new world.

CHAPTER VI

COLLEGE AND HEARTBREAK
CHANGSHA, HUNAN PROVINCE

1978 – 1982

I left Tianjin for college after the Lunar New Year in 1978. The first leg of the trip was three hours north to Beijing, where I changed trains for the twenty-three-hour ride south through three provinces to Changsha, the capital and largest city in Hunan Province. I brought only clothes and a quilt, all tied inside a large cloth. I told my mother I did not think I would need a quilt that far south in China, but she said, "That's okay, if it's warm you won't use it, and if it's cold you'll be thankful to have it." In fact, because Changsha is just south of the Yangtze River, and most buildings were not heated, I ended up using that quilt many months out of the year.

My father could only afford a hard seat ticket for me, which, at twenty-six *yuan*, cost him half a month's salary. I sat for the long ride on a wooden bench that I shared with two other travelers, but to have a seat of my own, instead of standing for the entire trip, felt luxurious. The ride was long, yet not the worst of the options. There was another train with many more stops, which took fifty-two hours to reach Changsha. Anyway, it did not matter how long the journey, nor how hard the seat was, I was so happy I could not even sleep. I wore a nice shirt given to me by my uncle, and when the conductor asked, "Where are you going, young man?" I proudly told him I was off to college.

Passengers seated nearby overheard our conversation and began speaking to me. Most people traveling were friendly simply because, at the time, the ability to take such a journey was an enormous privilege. Passengers needed a permit to travel and were required to declare a specific purpose for travel. I remember their curiosity and regard for me. The conductor went out of his way to be respectful and kind, bringing me extra hot water throughout the trip. Like everyone else, I had my own lidded tin teacup, which was filled after each train stop from a large metal pot insulated with a padded jacket to protect the conductors from burning their hands.

Throughout the trip, I took out books to review and study, but more, to display my work ethic and self-discipline. As someone on my way to college, it was important to be polite, to exhibit the manners of the educated, and to never, ever use foul language, a philosophy which I follow to this day. It is not, and never has been, in my nature to swear. Maybe the word "damn"—that would be my limit. Only the most exemplary behavior befits a scholar. Confucius taught that those who use their brains shall lead, and those who use their hands shall follow, a principle by which all Chinese live, and why the college entrance exam still retains a place of such high status in Chinese culture. This test is the way young men and women can lift themselves out of the working masses, use their intelligence, and lead.

The very language of education reinforces this philosophy:

Primary school is called *xiao xue,* meaning small study.
Middle school is called *zhong xue,* meaning mid-level study.
High school is called *gao zhong,* meaning higher than mid-level study.
But college takes a leap ahead; it is called *da xue*—giant study.

These terms indicate both the effort involved and the level of learning. Nobody can just jump into college. Everyone who attends must be admitted via the entrance exam and only that exam. There is no review of other work done, community service, nor character assessment. Everyone is permitted to take the exam three times, but if the score is still not high enough for admission, that individual will never have a leadership position in China. Counselors and even ambulances wait outside the government offices that post exam results, because young people who do not make the cut are so despondent, some are driven to suicide on learning their outcome. It is that intense.

Changsha is the capital and hub of the Hunan province, a bustling city known for spicy food. Mao was born in Hunan province, in the village of Shaoshanchong, and received part of his education in Changsha. When the train arrived there, I received a warm welcome from school volunteers who came to greet me and other students arriving to attend any of the city's thirty universities. I needed to show my acceptance letter before boarding the bus that would take me to the Railway College, and though students were arriving from all over the country, I found two others in the Foreign Language Department who had also traveled from Tianjin.

The Railway Ministry had eight colleges throughout the country. In Changsha, the college served 2,200 students in a three-story, concrete building. I lived in a dormitory, where I shared a room and three bunk beds with five roommates. Our belongings were stored at the end of our beds, and we all used the same desk placed in the middle of the room. Dormitories were separate from the education building, as was the library, where I spent all my weekend days. I was so hungry to learn, it was my entire focus during those three years.

I remained dependent on my father for the same essentials he had helped me purchase when I was at the farm. Every month he would send me two *yuan* for paper, envelopes, stamps, kerosene for my lamp, and other incidentals like soap and toothpaste. I also needed to spend ten cents whenever I took a shower. College students were not allowed to do any work other than schoolwork. The government-owned academies covered the cost of classes, books, and housing—and we were given coupons worth 10.50 *yuan* (about U.S. $5.00) to cover all our food for a month. But many of the foreign language students in my class had their own money to spend. One woman was a deputy minister, and a private car dropped her off every day. Others came to college as salaried teachers who continued to get paid with the understanding that, after graduating, they would return to their schools.

In China, a college class is named for the year the students are admitted to college, not the year of graduation as is the custom in many countries. The class of 1977, as we were called, was nationally renowned for several reasons. First, it marked the beginning of change, because for the first time in ten years, people could take the exam. This meant hope for overcoming difficult situations, for becoming educated and changing the way we lived. The class of 1977 allowed highly talented young people to enter a variety of fields and to make their marks professionally in China, as well as in the West. They have been the core of leadership in China, academically, politically, and scientifically for the past fifty years. This class has been the major force for China becoming a global power.

Because the college entrance exam had not been offered since 1965, 5,700,000 young people from all over the country took the entrance exam late in 1977. Only 270,000 were admitted, just 4.8 percent of those who tried, the lowest college entrance rate in China before or since. People who remember that period still associate the class of 1977 with hard work, good luck, and leadership in all fields.

I was one of the youngest students at Changsha and definitely one of the poorest. In general, the foreign language students were the elite in the college, and they arrived at the dining room first to buy the best lunches. Twenty-five-*fen* meals (about fourteen U.S. cents at the time) contained a substantial amount of meat. Twenty-*fen* meals (about eleven cents) had a little meat, fifteen-*fen* meals eggs or tofu, and five- or ten-*fen* meals were mostly beans, cabbage, and other inexpensive and pickled vegetables. I did not want my classmates to know I did not have enough money to eat what they were eating, so I always came late and acted disappointed to find all the good food was gone. The only meals left would be the cheap vegetable ones I could afford, along with two pieces of bread for four cents. Once or twice a week I enjoyed a twenty-cent meal with small bits of meat. Regardless, it was a hot meal prepared by someone else and served to me, a major improvement over the farm. The pride I felt in being a good student mattered far more than what I ate.

My lack of funds also inhibited my social life. A beautiful river ran through town some miles from campus, and couples would go there to be alone. It cost ten cents to travel there by bus and ten cents to return. For me and a date, that would mean spending forty cents just to get there. Then I would be expected to buy a popsicle, and the best of those cost five cents. Again, I would need to get one for my date and one for myself, but I had no extra money for that. As such, I never really dated, though I remember a sweet girl who would give me her extra food coupons to help me out.

There was also a pleasant female foreign language student who sat next to me in English literature class and because we were both dismissed from class at the same time, we would walk together after class. We started practicing short story recitation with each other as we walked. Soon thereafter, a Communist Party member "monitor" in my class reported our walking together to the department political commissar as unacceptable behavior. I argued that it was a small class, we had been assigned seats near one another, we were dismissed at the same time, and we were doing schoolwork. The commissar asked why I did not choose to study with a man. Although my female friend and I walked several feet apart from one another, I was told it was inappropriate and he warned that we should not get any closer. There was so much control and suspicion, yet the leaders themselves married classmates much younger than themselves.

I loved learning, but it was still China, and there were still rules. Another incident that got me in trouble involved the lights-out rule. The electric lights in the dormitories were supposed to be turned off at ten o'clock every night. At the start of college, I was substantially behind the older, more experienced foreign language students and worked hard to catch up to them academically. When the lights went out, I sat under a makeshift tent I had devised out of a tobacco box. I turned on my small kerosene lamp and continued to study well into the night.

The same Communist Party member who reported my walking with the fellow female student happened to be one of my roommates. He told me I needed to turn off my light and go to bed at ten. I argued that I was studying hard for "The Revolution" and was not disturbing anyone. But to appease him and follow the rule, I moved into the communal bathroom where dimmed lights stayed on through the dark hours. It was a stinky, uncomfortable place with a long ditch in the floor and little else. But I was willing to endure anything to catch up to the others in my class. I had never experienced being behind in school before.

Again, I was reported. This time I went to the dean, who was also a foreign language professor and knew I was a good student. I asked him to please let me continue studying in the loo, and he said he would "make an exception." But soon other students were also studying in the low light of the bathroom at night. That is how I started a trend.

The foreign language department was equipped with a state-of-the-art lab. Wearing headphones, we could listen to spoken words, repeat them, and listen to how we sounded. In this way, we were constantly improving our pronunciation.

We all came to class with different dialects from all over China. On the first day of class, the professor told us, "Forget everything you've learned in the past," and told us to recite the entire English alphabet. Then she declared we had failed the test and sent us to begin working in the lab.

The first year of study was mostly mechanics. I had to learn to exercise different muscles in my mouth to produce sounds that were not part of the Chinese language. I bought a small hand mirror, the kind women use to apply lipstick, and practiced moving my mouth to form the words. It is challenging when you have not used your tongue and lips in the way that the language demands, and, to a degree, I had to unlearn what I had previously learned. English is a complex language.

The oral English teacher was only four years older than I and spoke beautiful British English. Curious about him, I researched to discover that he grew up in a farming community in Rugao County in Jiangsu Province and was one of the few rural students selected to go to college in 1973, four years before the college exams had been reinstated. His name was Zhao Quan Chen and his skills were so exceptional—the best out of sixty students in his class—that he was sent to Great Britain to study before graduating from college in China. Because his story encouraged and inspired me, I went to his dormitory to introduce myself. Though surprised to see me at his door, he greeted me with a smile. "Tiehan, what can I do for you?" he asked. I told him I wanted to further introduce myself and recite a short story he assigned our class. He invited me inside, offered me a seat, then poured me a cup of tea. "I'm all ears," he said.

I proceeded to recite the story *The Barking Dog Does Not Attack*. It goes like this:

A grandpa and his grandson hear a dog barking ferociously and the grandson is afraid. "Don't worry," the grandpa says. "Don't you know that a barking dog does not attack?" The boy seemed to understand this, but still he wondered. "Grandpa," he said, "now I know a barking dog does not attack, and you know a barking dog does not attack—but does the dog know he will not attack?"

This was one of a hundred stories we learned to improve our spoken English, which I was practicing with my female classmate. These stories had a rhythm that made them easy to memorize. I got an A in the class and Zhao Quan Chen and I became lasting friends.

I began classes on March 1st, and by summer break, I was happy and ready to make the trip back home. I remember that summer as one of my happiest times in China. Although the ticket was expensive, my parents were worried about me living in the south, eating rice and spicy food. This time on the train I wore my college student badge and felt the respect of my fellow travelers. At home I recognized my parents' pride and their delight with my accomplishments.

During my four-week break, I tutored high school students in the neighborhood who had not passed the entrance exam and visited with neighbors who regarded me as a kind of celebrity in their midst. I had become an unofficial example of rising out of poverty, and I willingly accepted that role. I felt

I had earned it, that I had worked hard, and there was justice in my success. I also made a trip back to the farm to visit my friends. They were shocked that I would return, but they were important to me, too. I had lived with them for three-and-a-half years, and truthfully, I have never forgotten any of them. I brought dried noodles, which were a luxury, and candies for the kids.

In my second year at the Railway College, the language students were taught by three native English speakers, one each from the United States, the United Kingdom, and New Zealand. This made an enormous difference in our learning. The American teacher, Jesse Parker, who was only three years older than I, Harvard-educated and curious about Chinese culture, chose for me the English name Brian (meaning strong-willed), which I carry to this day. My last name, Chang, is my father's name, changed from Zhang to make it easier for Westerners to read. Chinese names that began with Z, X, and J were typically altered so that the spelling reflected their pronunciation. Historically this has been done with names from all over the world to make them easier for English speakers to say, spell, and remember. Having an English name in my class was a tool for learning the language and for identifying with the names in English literature.

Early in the school year, Jesse Parker asked if I was free on Saturday morning to accompany him to the farmers' market and help him buy produce. We met at the school gate and went to the market, where I translated for him. I enjoyed this first opportunity to translate, and it was a pleasure being in his company. After the market we went to his apartment, which was unlike anything I had seen before. He lived in what was called the Foreign Expert Building in his own apartment, with a private bathroom, air-conditioning, and a portable water boiler in the hallway for hot water day and night. I was in awe at such a level of luxury.

The next day I was asked by a commissar why I went to the Foreign Expert Building with Jesse Parker. I said, "Because he asked for my help at the market." "But you didn't get permission," he scolded. I replied that I did not know that I needed permission. Then I was given a warning. "We assign people to help," I was told. When Jesse Parker asked me to translate at the market for him again, I declined, explaining that I did not have permission according to the college rules. He got angry, of course. As an American, he was not used to such irrational constraints.

When Jesse went to the dean to question the rule, it caused more trouble for me. I was summoned to the commissar's office, who wanted to know why I told the American English teacher about the rule. "That rule was for Chinese," he said. I argued that I could not lie to my professor. The commissar was speechless. "Pay attention to where you stand politically," he said.

I realized then that I would not be given an elite job after graduation, like translating for the government or going abroad, because I could not be trusted to follow rules and dictates. I had studied at night after lights out, had walked with a girl, and I had failed to ask permission to help my American professor. The commissars who touted these rules had also graduated from college, but in the years when all you had to do was show up and do what you were told. They did not understand someone like me, working beyond myself to learn and to do well. Looking back, I find it interesting that I argued for logic and reason. I did not act like someone who was afraid of breaking the rules.

That year I decided not to go home for Lunar New Year to allow myself more time to move ahead and excel in my studies. In addition, it was a long and expensive trip. So I stayed at school. I was the only student who did.

On the second day of the Lunar New Year, an official from my department came to inform me that I had a telegram. The only time people got telegrams was for very good news, like getting into college, or for very bad news. Telegrams were expensive and never used except in emergencies. This telegram stated that my mother was sick, and I needed to return home immediately. It did not explain the details. The train ride was twenty-six hours long, and for the first six hours I stood, as there were no seats available. I only hoped that my mother would be alive when I got to Tianjin.

I arrived to learn that a blood vessel had burst in her head, maybe a stroke or some type of aneurysm. She had survived and was taken to the hospital. However, my mother had been denied admission because our family had no connections to people of privilege and knew no persons in key positions. We lacked *guanxi*. As a result, my mother was left on a bed in the hospital hallway with minimal medical assistance. I began contacting everyone I knew who might have some connection that would enable my mother to be officially admitted to the hospital so she could be moved from the hallway into a room. I even knelt on the floor begging a friend's father to help us obtain a certificate required to purchase the medicines she needed. Without that certificate, I could not buy her medicine. I was desperate, but nothing worked.

While my mother lay barely attended and dying, the top floor of the hospital remained mostly empty, awaiting a party official or high-ranking individual who might need medical attention. Without connections, my mother was left to whatever the doctors and nurses could do for her in the hallway—which was not enough to save her life.

I did get to see her alive and hold her hand, and I am forever thankful for that. She smiled and even tried to say something to me. I believe she waited for me to arrive before she passed away, though I cannot prove it. She died young, five months short of turning fifty-four. It brings me great sadness to this day because it did not have to be that way. With the right treatment, she would have had a chance to recover. We then had to transport her lifeless body back home using a long wheelbarrow contraption. Everything we did in those days was difficult. Yet we accepted it; we did not know any other way. We did not think about problems, or dwell on them, and I do not remember anyone being depressed. Maybe we just did not have time. People did not tell stories of the past or the hardships they had endured. There are many things about my mother I did not know, because we were just so busy surviving.

She was the light of the room, compassionate and truthful, and beautiful in every way. She was genuine and did not hide her happiness or her tears, which was why she was so well-liked and people were drawn to her. We cremated my mother and buried her in a small crypt as was the custom.

I returned to college and continued working hard. But back in Tianjin, my father's health began to decline. He had relied on my mother to maintain the household—to make meals, wash clothes, keep things clean—and had never developed the skills to perform such tasks. He was a good man of a chauvinistic era when men earned the money and women did everything else, and he was lost without her. A year and a half after my mother's death, my father resigned his job to open a position in the city for my youngest sister. She had graduated from high school by then, and, since our other two sisters had the city jobs allotted to our family of four children, she would have been sent to work in the countryside. My father's retirement created a city slot for my sister, who was then able to remain and work in Tianjin.

Without a routine, my father's health further deteriorated. He collected a pension of forty *yuan* a month, but he smoked, which cost thirteen Chinese pennies a pack. He did not eat well and was lonely. I wrote to him once a month, and though he did not tell me how tough things were for him, I sensed it. "Don't worry about me," he would say. But I worried about him all the time.

Through my years at the Railway College, I met three Americans who influenced me, changed my life, and remain friends to this day. My English language professor, Jesse Parker, is one of these friends. The second is Roland Fischer, who was teaching English at Nankai University in Tianjin when I was in college. I was introduced to him by a fellow Changsha foreign language student whose father taught at Nankai University with Roland Fischer, and when we rode the train home together, she invited me to participate in the English discussions that Roland facilitated. He continued to support me in my efforts to learn English and was later instrumental in my journey to America.

My third lifelong American friend is André Gillet, whom I met when he and a delegation from International Multifoods attended the Canton Fair in Guangzhou the summer of 1979. A group of students from the Railway College were assigned to be translators and tour guides to this delegation at the import-export fair. We were housed in a local high school where we slept on top of the desks and ate our meals in the canteen. All of us were excited to practice English with people who knew no Chinese, and who came to the trade show from all over—Africa, Canada, New Zealand, and the United States. China was just opening for international business. Mao's rules against foreign relationships had economically damaged the country, so in December 1978, Deng instituted an Open Door Policy to allow business with other countries to try and stimulate the Chinese economy.

I was told that an American delegation would be visiting for five days and that I was to do whatever I could to keep them happy. A driver had been assigned to pick the businessmen up at the airport, but he was late. It is important to mention that drivers in China then had power because most people in the country did not drive cars. Cars were scarce, and those who knew how to drive and fix cars held status above even a college graduate. The professions at the top were doctors (because they dispensed medicine), police (because they had power), sailors (because they traveled and could purchase foreign goods), and drivers. That day the driver chose to be late, and when we got to the airport, the delegation was upset about having to stand in the heat, waiting for their ride.

I apologized and escorted them to the Orient Hotel, the best hotel in Guangzhou at that time. When I gave them their hotel keys, these men realized that they were expected to share rooms. No, this was not acceptable to them. These were not people who shared rooms. I explained it was the rule, but the answer in return was, "Says who?" They were infuriated. I went to the hotel manager and told him that the delegation was serious—they did not want to share rooms. The manager said they could have individual rooms, but it would cost them extra money, which was irrelevant to the Americans.

This was a total eye-opener for me. These people preferred convenience and privacy over saving money. It was a completely different way of thinking. I came from a culture where we never had enough, where we grabbed bits of vegetables that had fallen off the cart. I saved anything I could save, especially money. I had spent my entire life calculating how to save money, and these people calculated how to be comfortable. They came out of a culture of abundance. Each man wanted a room of his own and did not think twice about what it would cost for that to happen.

Because time was important to this group, I did not want them to be routinely waiting for their driver. Each day all of us translators were given packages of high-quality cigarettes as gifts. I decided to pass along my cigarettes to our driver, telling him, "Look, these men are elderly and overweight, and we cannot leave them out in the sun waiting for you." I continued to bring the driver cigarettes every day, and from then on, everything went smoothly. He drove right to the door whenever he picked us up and even called me "Master!" Under my care, the Americans were treated much better than when they visited Beijing.

André Gillet was one of the men in that delegation, and at some point, we had a conversation. He asked me about my background and family, and, on the last day, he asked me to take him to the Friendship Store so he could purchase a watch for his son. He found a very nice watch, two-toned, gold-plated, and automatic. He asked me to try it on to see if it would fit his son. "My son is about your size," André told me, though when I met his son years later, I chuckled to myself when I saw that he is six feet tall and not at all my size. On the last day, André quietly gave me the watch with his thanks. It was an expensive watch costing more than 200 *yuan*, and feeling it was something I could not accept, I respectfully declined. I believed gifts should be earned, and that I had not earned such a precious and expensive gift, though I understood André's kind gesture. When André insisted, I thought of my father who had supported me all my life and was still sending me two *yuan* every month. I decided to keep the watch knowing I would give it to my father. That was the only way I would accept it, though I did not tell André at the time.

Brian and André Gillet in the 1980s

When I returned to Tianjin that summer, I gave my father the watch. When he asked how I got it, I explained about the kind man from the United States who gave it to me as a gift. My father had never owned a watch in his life. Now he would wear this exquisite gold-plated, automatic watch and proudly tell everyone, "My son gave it to me." I heard him say that then, and I hear him say that now. It was the only material gift I would ever give my father, and he almost never took it off. When he died and was cremated, my sisters knew to let the watch remain with him. It was more than a watch. André offered me this special gift, which I used to honor my father. The watch was a symbol of the human chain of giving and caring.

My father deserved honor, as did my mother. I think of her quiet support for my schoolwork when I lived at home. No matter how late I studied, she waited up for me. In the summer, when I studied outside in the heat, she made mung bean soup, sweetened with a pinch of sugar, to prevent me from getting heatstroke. I went back into the house to find a bowl of it, sweet and satisfying, waiting for me. She also made sweet wheat flour triangles and kept them warm. To this day I can taste the sweetness of my mother's mung bean soup and the buns and triangles, loving gestures of her understanding and caring, keeping vigil for me even when I did not return until midnight because I was busy learning the chemistry chart or reciting an assigned poem over and over to myself. In so many ways, my parents let me know that they were always there with unconditional love. It made me who I am and led me to this unlikely life.

CHAPTER VII

Leaving China
Qiqihar, Heilongjang Province,
Shanxi Province, and Tianjin

1982 – 1984

I had hoped that after graduating from college, I would find work in Beijing that would be close enough to my father to help take care of him. Although I wondered about the type of job I would be assigned, I never believed it would be inferior, since college graduates were held in such high esteem. With a college degree, I would be considered an intellectual. Now ten million people graduate from college every year in China, with 20 percent of them unemployed, though they are not labeled "unemployed." They are considered "at temporary rest from employment," also known as "flexibly" employed. When I graduated, however, only one out of 100,000 people had a college degree. It is difficult to overstate how many doors unlocked for someone possessing a college degree at that time.

In those days China was a planned economy, where factors of geography, academics, and political favor were all considered when making job assignments. Those with high-ranking backgrounds were awarded the best jobs, of course, and one's city of origin also mattered. Those from Beijing were considered first for employment in and near Beijing and those from Shanghai for jobs in Shanghai. Because they were the most desired locations, graduates from other parts of China also wanted to be assigned jobs there. One of the women in my class, a Communist Party member, so badly wanted to work in Shanghai that she faked having cancer, telling the authorities that the only treatment available to her was in Shanghai. But by accepting a job in Shanghai, she displaced a Shanghai native, who was then bumped down to some remote area with dim job and life prospects.

Each assignment had the potential to disrupt the lives of many other students. The woman who lied about her health paid no consequences and did not die of cancer. But no one contested job assignments and we had absolutely no input. Only a few cities were preferred by college graduates, most of them in the north. We looked down on southern cities like Guangzhou, where the people spoke Cantonese, not Mandarin, which had been the official language of China since 1911, and they ate wildly exotic foods, from peacock to snake.

When I graduated, I was handed a folder containing my diploma and academic performance, an introduction letter to my new employer, and a sealed envelope containing my political assessment, which could not be opened except by the cadre at my assigned job. I took this folder with me to my assignment as an English teacher at a two-year college in Beijing for engineers who would become station heads or steel production supervisors. It was the job assignment I had hoped for; I would regain my urban registration, be close to my father, and, where I had once been at the bottom, I would advance to places that seemed limited only by the sky.

I reported to work, where I was warmly welcomed and informed that they were still in the process of recruiting the head of school. In the meantime, I was assigned to work as a teacher in one of the railway's thirty-one factories, where all of China's steam and electric engines, railway cars, rails, and signals were built. Instead of living in Beijing where I would have been close to my father, I was sent to the remote area of Qiqihar near the Siberian border, farther north than Mongolia, even farther than North Korea.

My students in Qiqihar were engineers from all over China, bright and hard-working people, who needed to learn enough English to read and translate operations and repair manuals for trains purchased from the United States. As part of China's move toward modernization and international trade, the country had replaced old steam engines that moved at only sixty kilometers an hour, with more than 100 locomotives purchased from General Electric. There was a need for workers who could understand the manuals and run the new trains, all part of the country's industrial modernization at that time. The students in my class had to leave their spouses and children for six months to receive this training.

Though I was far from my father, this was a good job. I found it easy to teach people who were intelligent and motivated. However, learning English was a challenge for my students, who were in their thirties and forties. There were twenty students, seventeen men and three women, all older than I was. At first, I found the age difference awkward, because according to Confucius, a teacher is like a father. To equalize us, I gave each of my students an English name, just as Jessie

Parker had given me the name Brian. They loved it. It helped them feel like part of the language and culture, and when I spoke to any of them years later, they still used their English names, like William, Sam, and George.

We were all part of a changing industrial system, interested in gaining the skills to advance. I quickly realized that I wanted to continue my own education and get a master's degree, though I needed to work for two years to be eligible. I stayed in touch with Jesse Parker, who encouraged me to look for a scholarship to study in the United States. But at that time, I could not have obtained a personal passport for travel outside of the country. China issued only state passports, which were rare beyond the military or foreign service and highly coveted. At that time, I did not think about getting a graduate degree in the United States. It seemed too far-fetched.

In Qiqihar I got up earlier than my students to study and prepare for graduate school. I taught my group from nine until noon, then we took a break for two hours, which seemed odd to me. What was the purpose of two idle hours in the middle of the day? We resumed class from two to four thirty. In the evenings, there was little to do and no entertainment. It was a remote place, it was winter, and the sun set by five o'clock. We all stayed in the dormitory, or a guest house, located inside the vast factory where massive cargo train cars were produced.

Because my students were well-educated, we spent many evening hours discussing Beethoven, Shakespeare, Chaucer, and other scholarly topics. One of the students had studied at Moscow University. Another had a cassette of *Swan Lake*, which we would listen to—the four small swans and the light, beautiful music—there in the shadow of Mao. I felt my heart lift. The future seemed bright.

Although the work was challenging and the location remote, I was not lonely. Furthermore, I was making more money than I could have imagined just a few years earlier. As a first-year teacher, I earned forty-six *yuan* (about U.S. $26.00) a month, and sent thirty to my father, who was so proud of me. I also received additional stipends of around fifteen *yuan* a month for working in a remote part of the country.

After the six-month program in Qiqihar, I returned to Beijing to find that the academy where I had been assigned still had not hired an administrator. Finding a suitable leader would take time, I was told. It seemed I was not going to realize my almost perfect position. I was reassigned to Railway Ministry Yongji Locomotive Works, an electric locomotive factory of 11,000 employees in the western part of Shanxi province about 1,000 miles west of Beijing, in a county of 90,000 people that ranked as the poorest in that province. After arriving I reported to the guest house where my students and I were to live. My students arrived from all over China for six months of training from as far north as Manchuria and from southern and southwest provinces. Again, these were all highly educated engineers attending school to learn enough oral English to carry on simple conversations in English-speaking countries with the goal of producing specialized train cars such as those made by General Electric.

Classes lasted from eight thirty in the morning until four thirty in the afternoon, with one midday break, following the work schedule of Locomotive Works. At that time, the Railway Ministry owned thirty-one different factories, all of them enormous. Four factories produced locomotive engines and the other twenty-seven built all the other cars, including green cars, oil cars, cargo, passenger, and self-cleaning cars.

Again, the students were all older than I was and called me "Little Teacher Zhang." I felt at ease with them and respected them. In turn, they respected me. Once a month, most of them went home for a long weekend and brought back local food specialties native to their provinces, such as dates or peaches, which they shared with me. Like Qiqihar, there was little entertainment at night, so we sat together and talked about authors like Balzac, philosophers like Voltaire and Cao Xue Qin's *Dream of the Red Mansion*, a well-known eighteenth century Chinese novel. One fellow played the violin and, overall, these activities enriched our lives and gave our days meaning and significance. The time passed quickly until the break for the lunar holiday, when we enjoyed almost four weeks of vacation, then returned to school and continued classes into the spring months.

One day in April, I suddenly fell ill with a high fever, vomiting, and chills. I could hardly eat and was hospitalized at the Locomotive Works on-site hospital. But I did not get better. After three days, I still had a high fever and had developed jaundice. I was diagnosed with acute hepatitis A, a highly contagious disease that everyone dreaded in China at that time. Though I was quarantined, it was determined that I needed better medical treatment than the local hospital could provide. I was transported by train to Beijing in a hard berth compartment containing six seats, three bunk beds, and no doors. I wore a mask and was covered with a sheet, but nobody had been informed of my infectious condition except for the main conductor on the train. I received such special treatment because I was college-educated. Otherwise—seriously—I would have been put on a truck. The trip took twenty hours on a modern train that had been purchased from the United States. Traveling at 120 miles per hour, it went double the speed of older steam engines.

By the time I was taken to the Railway Ministry Beijing Bureau General Hospital, ranked as a first-class facility, I had been sick for four days. I was admitted, given treatment, and sent to a quarantine room in the infectious disease section of the hospital with three other hepatitis A patients, each in our own bed in four corners of the room, which was the size of a normal, small hospital room.

I was told I would be there for ten days to two weeks. No visitors were allowed, and we were quarantined in the room with a heavy chain and large lock barring the door. I was small enough to squeeze through the gap, but that would have broken the rules. It is not in my nature, but, more importantly, I did not want anyone else to get sick. There was no window in the room. There were toilets, but no bathing. This was the setting in a first-class hospital at that time. At mealtime, the door would be unlocked, and we would be given plates of food to eat in the room. We could hear the patients with schizophrenia in the corridor next to the infectious desease section crying, shouting, and breaking things day and night. Forget about peace and quiet in the hospital.

Though I missed my father and sisters terribly, I did not have the courage to tell them I was sick. Even later, I did not tell them. In China, hepatitis A is associated with malnourishment, caused by a lack of food and working too hard. I did not want my family to worry or feel guilty that I was sending half of my monthly salary to them. Anyway, why would I call them? They would have insisted on coming to see me, even though traveling between Tianjin and Beijing was not easy. They could not have come into my room, and I did not want them to see me like that. The person I missed the most then was my mother. If she had been alive, she would have made noodle soup for me. I longed for her and her noodle soup.

I remained in the hospital for fourteen days. Toward the end of my stay, I received a surprise visit from Zhao Quan Chen, my well-spoken Changsha English teacher and friend. When the nurse came to my room to announce I had a visitor, I saw him in the doorway. I walked to the door and he held out both hands to me through the space in the door. We shook hands for thirty seconds, but it seemed like a lifetime. We said hello and I cried. He told me he was terribly sorry for not coming sooner, but he did not know I was there. He had come to Beijing on a business trip and several of the other students from my college class invited him to dinner. It was through them that he learned of my illness.

"Is there anything I can do?" he asked me. I said no, but thanked him, then we made some small talk because a more meaningful conversation would have depressed me. The next day he came back again and brought cookies. Then he returned to Changsha. When we left, he wished me well and afterward we continued corresponding. But I did not see him again for thirteen years.

By that time, I had lived and worked in the United States for more than a decade and had advised him on how to do the same. He ended up coming to the U.S. and eventually received his PhD from the University of Buffalo in New York. Chen went on to become a tenured associate professor at Rutgers University and the Chair of the Organizational Behavior Department. I invited him to my wedding in 1996, when we were finally able to shake hands with one another again. We were not able to spend much time together at my wedding, but between friends like me and Chen, words are not important. We know what friendship means.

After Chen visited me in quarantine, I had to consider why none of the four classmates he had talked to at dinner had come to see me in the hospital. This is worth mentioning because of the Chinese cultural implications. In college, I was an equal to these people. My grades were as good as theirs, if not better. But I had rebelled in small ways, never willing to accept rules that made no sense or degraded me as a human being. For that reason, I was valued as a skilled employee, but not as a trusted employee. Of those four former classmates, three were working for the Railroad Ministry's Department of Foreign Affairs at the time. One had traveled overseas twice. The fourth colleague worked for the Loan and Financing Department, dealing directly with the United Nations and the War Bank. Their successes made them feel uncomfortable dealing with my difficulties. They were all facing bright futures and I was supposed to be part of that cohort.

Instead I was teaching English to engineers and now very ill with an infectious disease that bore a degree of negative stigma. It was not fair, and I never forgot it. But if I had enjoyed such a high-level position out of college, I would not have been motivated to leave China. My misfortune became my fortune. I realize that now.

When I was discharged, I moved back to the Railway Ministry guest house to await my next assignment. I wondered if my students were still waiting for me to finish their training but found out that my class had been canceled and the students sent home. There had only been a few weeks left of the training anyway. I was told to take it easy and was given a desk in the Railway Ministry offices in Beijing. Though I reported there every morning promptly at nine, I had no specific task or assignment, allowing me to spend the day studying for the Graduate Record Exams (GRE).

Whenever I was given a week off work, I went home to spend it with my dad. I washed his clothes, got him a haircut, took him to the public bathhouse, and we went out to dinner. Eating out was inexpensive then. We ate tasty dumplings and drank a jar of Chinese wine for a total of one *yuan*. It was obvious how proud he was of me. He wore the Railway Ministry bright blue uniform and the gold watch I had given him. He loved the watch so much, he would even ask the time just to look at it. He never inquired about my work. As far as he was concerned, I was guaranteed a bright future and having me back in Beijing was icing on the cake. I never told him how sick I had been.

We spent a wonderful week together, and I was full of hope, anticipating my next assignment. But when I returned, there was still no news. I was told to report to the education department to basically do nothing. I sat at the far end of a large room, making sure all the high-ranking officials' thermoses were full of hot water, then I would sit and do nothing. Such a job was a bragging point; being idle on the job in China was seen as a positive at the time. That is how upside-down things were. I was happy to do GRE simulations and read the Jack London stories I loved.

In the summer of 1983, I was informed that the academy would not be built. They had a difficult time finding a high-ranking person to fill the position, which was to be located twenty miles south of Beijing, near what is now the airport. Because it would require a long commute, nobody wanted the job. For my next assignment, I was to report to Han Xin Dian in the design department at the Railway Ministry Beijing February 7th Locomotive and Cars, an enormous factory facility that built both locomotive engines and cars. I was given a new certificate of work with my name, title, and place of employment, red-stamped to make it official. I was now a translator.

The facility employed and housed more than 12,000 workers and, like a small city, it offered all the services employees and their families would need from cradle to grave, including schools, a hospital, a grocery, department stores, and even a funeral home. I was given a small room and spent my time mostly translating operations and maintenance manuals from General Electric. The workload felt heavy at the time because nobody told me how many pages they expected me to translate in a day. There were considerable challenges figuring out and translating the terminology accurately. "Decoupling" the train is different than two dogs "decoupling"! I used many dictionaries to get it right. Because engineers had to know how to run and fix their trains, translation was not such a trivial task.

After a few months, I had translated all the manuals they had given me and was again summoned to the head of personnel. That is when I got the bad news: I was to be transferred from translating in the design department to teaching eighth-grade English in the facility's middle school. This immediately conjured images of Mr. Wu and of my own middle school teacher, both educated people, spending their days trying to discipline young people who did not want to learn.

I felt dejected. I had been teaching engineers and translating manuals, and now I had dropped several rungs on the status pole, so many it felt like being at the bottom. I struggled for days and did not even want to go home because I had no good news for my dad or anyone else. Of course, the demotion was circumstantial. I needed a job and the school needed an English teacher.

During that phase, I worked six days a week, and on the seventh day I went home to look after my father. I did not tell him about my work situation and he never asked. I had a college education, which was all that mattered. I had no other activities then and was not interested in dating. Because I had a college degree, I was considered "a catch," and was often approached with opportunities to meet girls. I always responded that I had a heavy domestic burden with an ailing father and three sisters, but really, it was a deliberate decision. I was not ready to get married and settle down. Instead I chose to focus on my education and career.

I was one of the few teachers who did not have a home. I moved into a dormitory, in a room with bunk beds once again. This time there were two sets of bunk beds—one bed for my roommate, one for me, one for our belongings, and the other for a physics teacher who showed up to take a nap every afternoon. In the classroom, I quickly found out that at least half of my eighth-grade students did not care about the subject of English or the teacher. I was not the type of teacher to dispense useless threats or badger students to learn. Instead, I told the disruptive ones, "I don't care if you don't want to learn. Leave or take a nap." This surprised them. I never stooped to echoing the propaganda they were used to hearing from teachers. When I asked students to leave the classroom, they took their noise outside. I was told that I needed to educate them to be revolutionary successes. My answer to that was, "I don't know how to become a revolutionary success myself!"

I was sometimes reminded not to discipline students whose parents were high-ranking officials. Politics was everywhere. Over time the students responded well to my approach because it was so different. I stayed respectful. And at four in the afternoon, my time was all my own. I ate in the cafeteria and had time to read and prepare lessons in the evenings. I told my students who wanted to learn English to come to the playground at seven in the morning, and I would answer their questions and help with their pronunciation as they recited their stories to me in English.

After one semester of teaching eighth grade, I was reassigned to teach twelfth grade. Students of that age knew English was important for the college exam and were more eager to learn. I kept learning on my own as well, preparing to take the GRE. Education had transformed my life before, and I believed it could transform my life again. I realized that without a graduate degree my opportunities would be limited. In China at the time, the top job for someone with an English degree would have been working in the foreign affairs department of the Communist Party, the state council, or any of the ministries. In those jobs, I would have had the opportunity to travel and meet people from other countries. Foreign affairs jobs also offered generous perks that might include personal drivers or 800 *yuan* (about U.S. $400) to buy a tailored suit.

But minor rebellions in college, including my "unauthorized" relationship with Jesse Parker, had been documented in the employment file that followed me everywhere I went. Not being selected for the desirable jobs like my peers solidified my resolve to attend graduate school. Beijing University was considered the most prestigious place to study, but it tended to favor its own undergraduate students. Instead, I focused on the China Social Science Academy where I could major in American Studies. Jesse Parker was living in Beijing at that time, and when I told him about my decision to go to graduate school, he replied that if I wanted to study America and the English language, I should go to America, and he offered to help me find a scholarship. Despite being skeptical, I continued to meet with him often, and he gave me history books and literature to continue my studies. Many things had to come together before I could leave China to study in America. When I look back, every one of them seems like a miracle.

First came the idea. When I talked with Jesse Parker and read *Animal Farm* and *1984*—in secret, of course—I understood that freedoms existed, and life did not have to be so tightly controlled by the government. Jesse was from Boston and helped me apply to graduate school at Northeastern, where I was accepted. But the scholarship was only partial and excluded room and board, making it unaffordable for me. Then André Gillet, who lived in Minnesota, facilitated my application to Hamline University Law School in St. Paul, Minnesota, where I was given a full scholarship contingent on my passing the law school entrance exam and studying law. However, the Chinese government denied me an exit visa to study at Hamline because they considered it a "religious" school. At the time, China did not encourage college graduates to leave and study in other countries, especially not law at a "religious" school.

I wrote an emotional letter to André thanking him for his help and influence and explained why I was denied approval by the Chinese government. But André was as determined as I was. He approached the University of Minnesota, and within a few weeks, I received an acceptance letter and full scholarship to attend graduate school with a major in American Studies. I reapplied to the Chinese government and received approval. But obtaining a passport was to be its own ordeal.

On February 7, 1984, I was working at Locomotive Works, assigned directly to the design department, on loan as a teacher to its affiliated school. The passport application had to come from Locomotive Works on my behalf because individuals were not allowed to apply directly at that time. To further complicate the passport application process, I needed approval from two bosses: the design director, who was my supervisor, but the head of the school was also a boss. There was always so much bureaucracy and control. I ended up waiting three long months for the passport application process, worrying about it every day. Finally, in May of 1984, I received approval. I immediately had my photo taken there at the factory, which provided all the necessities and then some. After that it was time to apply for a visa to enter the United States.

I arrived at the U.S. Embassy, again expecting the kind of resistance I had known all my life. During the interview, the consular officer asked me if I was a Communist, and I said no. He asked me if I would return to China after graduating, and I told him I did not know, which was an honest, but risky answer. Such an answer could imply intentions beyond studying. When he asked what I would be doing in the United States, I told him about my scholarship to the university. "Congratulations," he said to me. "Go and do something for yourself."

I was stunned. The entire interview took only minutes, and when I walked out to the waiting room so quickly, looking so happy, the people there, anxiously awaiting their turn, regarded me like a celebrity. Most interviews were long, and, not all of them ended well. People often hired consultants to coach them on the visa process because it was typically quite complex. Applicants might emerge from their interview glum or even swearing. But I believe the consular found my honest answers refreshing. That was the first indication that I was going to a great country with opportunities I would never have experienced in China.

As the pieces began to fall into place, and this far-fetched dream of studying in America became more real, the prospect of leaving my father weighed on me heavily. After I obtained my visa, we had a heart-to-heart conversation. I told him how concerned I was about him, that I did not have to go, and that I could postpone my scholarship and stay in Tianjin or Beijing teaching school. He became angry and said, "You want to make me proud." He said this was the dream I wanted and the dream he wanted for me. "Your mother didn't see you graduate from college, but I did," he said, "and now you go to graduate school in a country where the only limit is the sky."

Those were his exact words, which I hear him saying even now. He told me to do great things and to honor the ancestors who made this happen for me. Chinese people, especially the underprivileged, believe that those who went before do good for you, perhaps as a reward for their own sacrifices. My father told me to thank my grandparents for this opportunity to go to the United States, the most desirable place, a beacon of freedom, of technological advancement and military might. The most prominent Chinese scholars and scientists had all been educated in the United States. Nothing could be greater, and by going there, I would make my father and my whole family proud.

With this in mind, I proceeded with my plans to leave China. But I faced yet another challenge, one I had not foreseen: the plane ticket. It cost close to $1,000 to fly from China to the United States, and my entire life savings totaled 400 *yuan* (which converted to 200 U.S. dollars at the time). I did not know what to do, so I decided to get another job. I was earning fifty-six *yuan* each month (approximately thirty-two U.S. dollars at that time) and could have saved thirty-six of that for a total of just more than 400 *yuan* in a year's time. But at this rate, it would have taken me almost three years.

Then I got an idea—possibly from Jack London or some other adventure author I had read in my English studies. I took a long-distance bus to the Port of Xing Gang in Tianjin, went to a shipping company there, and asked to speak with a manager. The place was guarded, but I believe I was allowed inside because I had a passport and an intelligent way of speaking. I remember the manager as a very decent man. I explained my situation, my scholarship and inability to get to the United States. I told him that I wanted to work on a cargo ship in exchange for passage. I was willing to do anything—cook or scrub floors, anything. I said I was strong and could carry fifty kilos on my back.

He regarded me in amazement. "Where did you come up with that idea? Did you read that in some novel?" That is actually what he asked me. And though he was intrigued, there was no possibility of circumventing all the paperwork and approvals required to get someone on a ship. Because everything required a stamp of approval, too many stamps would be needed from too many government departments for me to travel by ship to the United States.

I was devastated. I had no way of getting to the University of Minnesota. I wrote this to André Gillet. I told him my fantastic tale of approaching the shipping company. I thanked him for everything he had done, told him that I would continue to work and save money, and that I would come to the United States in a few years. My visa was good for only six months, but my passport would last five years. I asked André to extend my gratitude to the University of Minnesota and to tell them to give my scholarship to someone else in need. Feeling powerless and stuck, I experienced many sleepless nights.

Soon after that, André's assistant wrote back to tell me that they understood my dilemma, and while they appreciated my willingness to work, I should contact Northwest Airlines' Shanghai office. A ticket had been arranged for me to travel on standby, all arranged by the Public Relations Department of André's employer, International Multifoods, and Northwest Airlines.

Today I understand the inner workings of public relations in large companies, corporate citizenship, giving back to the community, and other generous philanthropies. But living all my life in a Communist country with little food or goodwill, this gesture was completely unfamiliar to me. It was unthinkable that I would be given a ticket with no strings attached, 100 percent free. I was suspicious in the beginning. Why was everyone being so nice to me?

But it does not take long to accept such unconditional and unselfish goodwill. It touched my heart. Most importantly, it changed my mind about the kind of person I wanted to be.

With everything in place, I needed to face the fact of leaving my father. He was not talkative like my mother was, and I have always been, so we sat together before I left, mostly in silence. I reminded him I did not have to go just then, that I could delay my trip if he needed me. But after I said that he swore at me to "get the hell out of here and do great things." I had never heard my father swear before. He had such dignity all his life. But his pride in me ran deep, as did his hope for my future.

I understood the pleasure my father had telling people that his son was a college graduate, and how I had been teaching in

Beijing, helping engineers to learn English. I knew he loved it when others asked about me. When I was a child, he and my mother would argue over which one of them would attend the annual parent-teacher conference where my good grades were publicly posted. He had supported me all the way, sent me two *yuan* a month for the three-and-a-half years I was at the farm, and all though college. It was a large sum of money, but he gave it without qualm. He introduced me to Mr. Wu and bought me a radio to learn English in the countryside.

Both morally and monetarily, he had always supported me. I knew, and I believe he knew, that my success was also his success. He made the choice in his life to give up so much for me and to invest in my future. It did not come easily, as such sacrifices never do, but his willingness to save and help me is my model. I always make the same choice of saving to invest in those I love.

Never in my life had my father asked how I was doing in school. He always assumed I would do well. That was how much faith he had in me. I remembered the visits we made to Mr. Wu's, when he and his wife would speak to me in their perfect English, and I would translate for my father. He had such pride and excitement. Leaving my father in 1984, I was not sure I would ever see him again. We both recognized the reality of his age and poor health and the long distance across the Pacific Ocean that would separate us.

To this day I carry the guilt of pursuing my own life and not staying in China to care for my father. Both of my parents were so kind. They only wanted the best for their children and made great sacrifices for us at the expense of their own physical and emotional health, being forced to endure public humiliation and often going hungry.

There is the Chinese story of an old man with his old horse who lived near the Great Wall. One day his horse wandered away, devastating the man when it did not return. But a week later the old horse returned with a whole herd of horses. The lesson learned is that you never know in the moment if something is happening for good or bad. If you can graduate from misfortune, it is good fortune. Luck finds itself. My father knew that. He wanted me to go because he believed it was for the best.

Relatives and friends came to the house for a goodbye party before I left. The Fischers arrived with a chocolate cake, which we had to cut with a cleaver as we owned no smaller knives. When I brought a piece of cake to my father, he asked, "What is this?" I told him it was cake. He said it did not look like cake, but he tried it. He separated himself from the party; he was not interested in drinking and conversation. On the day I departed for Shanghai, my father went on his customary morning walk, then spent the day with me. Our immediate family ate an early dinner of dumplings together, but when it was time to leave for the train station, my father stayed home.

I knew his health would continue to decline. He was a dignified and proud man, and he would not let his son-in-law or my sisters help him with the intimate aspects of hygiene. Without me he would struggle to take care of himself. I told him I would call so we could still talk on the telephone.

I boarded the evening train for Shanghai, this time with a berth so that I could sleep on my journey. There were only two flights from Shanghai to Seattle each week, but I got a stand-by seat on my first attempt. Transcontinental planes at that time were rarely full. I had never flown before and found the experience breathtaking. Below me I saw Shanghai, the

Leaving China and saying good-bye to Rachel and Roland Fischer

most modern city in China, then and now, and the Yangtze River flowing into the East China Sea. It all felt so poetic, and my imagination ran wild. What was ahead? What would happen? I felt such freedom, and wandered around the plane listening to other passengers who stood in small groups chatting. I remember asking the flight attendant how much a beer cost. "There's no charge," she said, "but you can pay extra if you want!" Northwest Airlines offered three brands of beer on that flight—a Chinese beer, a Dutch beer, and Budweiser—and I ordered the Budweiser. I wanted the American brand, whatever it was.

I asked the flight attendant if I could move to an empty seat by the window and ended up staring out the window the entire flight. I could not sleep, and as the sky grew dark, I watched the red light flashing on the end of the airplane's wing. I was mesmerized, lost in thought and anticipation.

When I was a child, I was given Mao's *Little Red Book* full of sayings and rules of the Communist Party. Leaving China in November of 1984, I had a different little red book, a passport, granting me the freedom to live a new life.

CHAPTER VIII

Culture Shock and Sorrow
Minneapolis, Minnesota

1984 – 1988

When I landed in Minneapolis, I was greeted at the gate by André Gillet and his ten-year-old grandson, who was waving an American flag. This touched me. I have kept that flag on my desk throughout the years, a memento of my welcome arrival here. Because the dormitories at the University of Minnesota were closed for the Thanksgiving holiday, arrangements had been made for me to stay at the home of Betty and Joe Anderlik, who provided my first experience of life in America.

The Anderliks were an inspiration. Though both had humble backgrounds, Joe ran a successful company of 400 employees, and together they had raised three children, all grown adults by the time I met them. They were active volunteers who opened their beautiful home on Turtle Lake to foreign students like me. When I asked why they welcomed foreign students into their home, they explained that they loved to travel, and hosting students from other countries had broadened their children's education.

Immediately I felt the difference between the world where I had spent the first years of my life and the one I now inhabited. The Anderliks put me up in a bedroom with my own bathroom, which was an unbelievable luxury. The first morning there, I woke up early to go out for a walk and explore their neighborhood, but after making my way around Turtle Lake, I came back to find their door locked. I had never encountered a locked door in my life. Nobody in China locked a door; we did not even have locks. We owned nothing we thought anyone would want to steal, there was very little crime, and the government discouraged privacy and boundaries of any kind.

I had no idea what this locked door meant. Was I not welcome? Had I already offended the Anderliks in some way? My mind was racing 100 miles an hour. I knocked on the door, but nothing happened. There was a doorbell, but at that time, I did not know what such a thing was. It never occurred to me to push a little button by the door. Luckily Betty Anderlik passed by a window and saw me waving at her. She apologized as she let me back in the house.

My next shock came when they took me to a suburban shopping center. I had never seen so many cars in one place. When I left China, there were no private cars, none. And here was a whole lot full of cars. I thought maybe a national congress was being held there. That is when I learned that in the American suburbs, it is not one car for each family, but one car for each person in the family.

We entered Rainbow Foods, which did not resemble any grocery store I had known. The place was large and well-lit with an abundance of food openly displayed. And so many apples! I had no idea there were that many kinds of apples. I remember asking Betty, "Can I pick one up?" and she laughed. "Do you think someone else will pick it up for you?" We did not need coupons to buy food and could purchase whatever we wanted and as much as we wanted without restriction. I had never had such an experience with food. After Rainbow, we went to Byerly's food store, where the floors were carpeted and chandeliers hung from the ceiling. In a grocery store! Not only did we not need coupons, but there were no store attendants watching to make sure we did not steal. I realized then that in America there is an assumption you will not steal. There was so much food, so many choices and an underlying assumption of good; that in general, people will not dishonor the "code of trust." I cannot overemphasize what a major change in the way of thinking this was for me. When people grow up in a society void of trust, it is difficult to comprehend such openness.

On the first Sunday, my hosts, who were devout Catholics, took me to church with them. I had not ever been in a church, and though I tried to keep up with what was happening, I did not understand the content. The kneeling and movement confused me, and when I followed my hosts to Communion, I was stunned that wine was being served for breakfast. And so little bread! That evening I had my first meaningful discussion about religion, which was all very new to me. As I have said before, Mao wanted no competition from organized religion for the loyalty of the Chinese people.

So much happened in my early days in Minnesota. An administrator at the university asked me if I preferred a roommate who was Caucasian or one from an Asian country. I said I wanted to learn as much English as I could. I was, after all, an American Studies major. As a result, I was assigned to share a dormitory room with an undergraduate named Dave Janiszewski, who is still a close friend to this day. The day I moved in, Dave was out skiing, and I was greeted by his girlfriend, now wife, Janet, who lived in the female wing of the dorm. She was gracious, and after I asked her where I could put my clothes, she shoved Dave's things to one side and offered me half of the closet.

The classes I took tended to be large, and I was immediately struck by the lack of assigned seating. At the Railway College, I was told where to sit and who to sit with, what classes I would take and when I would take them. There were no electives, no freedom to change courses or skip classes. In China, all students stood when the teacher entered the room. But here everything was different. I saw students taking naps and looking at pictures, talking to each other, and registering only for classes in the afternoons so they could sleep all morning. The level of freedom and choice was astonishing.

I spent the first semester in chronic culture shock, and the dining hall was no exception. My room and board included three meals a day, multiple choices for each meal, and all I wanted to eat. A chicken sandwich intended for one person was made with a whole chicken breast. In China, we bought the smallest pieces of meat, then asked the shopkeeper to give us a fatty cut to use the oil from the fat for cooking. When Dave and Janet ordered a pizza one Friday night, I was puzzled, asking them, "Why did you buy that when we have all we can eat in the cafeteria?" They said they were tired of the cafeteria food. "This pizza tastes better than the dorm pizza," they told me. They were willing to spend money on food just to have variety. This, too, was new to me.

Though I found the dormitory food tasty and interesting, I did sometimes miss the food I had known in China. When the cafeteria had chop suey night, I encountered an odd take on Chinese food. The phrase *chop suey* literally translates as "leftover things," but the dormitory version of this—and of chow mein as well—was mostly celery in a kind of paste with dried noodles, a mix I had never seen before in my life. And it was always served with fortune cookies, which I had also never seen before in my life. Even when I had egg rolls, they were huge and full of cabbage, nothing like the crispy, artful ones I had prepared in China. But during my time at the university, I did not complain about food. I never had so much food available to me.

On Friday and Saturday nights, when other graduate students went out, I studied in the library. One nice young woman invited me to go to dinner with her, and I said, no, that I ate in the cafeteria, then went to the library. I did not realize at the time that she was, essentially, asking me on a date. "Aren't you getting tired of the cafeteria food?" she wanted to know. Again, I said no. I was not tired of having all that food that did not cost me any money. She asked me more than once and finally told me, in a nice way, that I was a "square." A square? A square is a place where people gather. A square is a geometrical shape. I looked it up in the dictionary to find out the kind of square she thought I was—old fashioned and boring!

I found the state of public bathrooms another shock. Wherever I went, there was always toilet paper, hot water, and soap, another kind of paper to wipe my hands, bright lights overhead, and heat or air-conditioning, depending on the season. I saw that public areas were routinely attended, much like private spaces. Public bathrooms were very dimly lit in China, and if there was toilet paper, in hotels for example, it would be on tiny rolls one quarter the size of the ones in the U.S. The authorities did not want to encourage the pilfering of light bulbs or toilet paper. In fact, there was a time when hotel guests would have to wait in the lobby during their checkout while the room was inspected for theft or broken items. If a towel was missing, it would be announced publicly in front of everyone in the lobby. If something was broken, even a cup, the guest would have to pay for it before being allowed to leave. There was never an assumption of goodwill. That is a fundamental difference between Communist China and the United States.

My strong curiosity drove me to venture out and take risks I did not calculate. I expanded my understanding of the country and made friends because I was not afraid to try. When André Gillet invited me to visit him at his office in downtown Minneapolis, I looked up the bus schedule and planned to get on the bus that would take me close to his office. I was not aware, however, that I needed the correct change, and that if I gave the bus driver a dollar for a twenty-five-cent ticket, I would not get any change back. When I learned this, I skipped that bus and found a change machine on campus to get quarters. Then I rode the next bus. When I arrived at André's office, he asked how I had managed to get there. "It wasn't that hard," I told him. "I took the bus."

Buses were a wonder to me. Most of the seats were not filled, so I never had to stand, the seats were comfortable, the temperature controlled against the weather and—remarkably—the buses ran on a schedule. In China, the bus would come when it came. Drivers there would wait until the bus was full before departing for the next stop. In the U.S., the bus leaves according to a timetable, whether full or empty.

In my first month, I had no U.S. dollars to do laundry, buy incidentals, or call my family in China. When I mentioned this to a counselor, he arranged a monthly stipend of $50 for me. The first month I received the stipend, I sent $40 to my father and phoned him. He had no telephone, so I had to call the public phone near his house and arrange with whomever answered for him to be there when I called back fifteen minutes later. He was excited to hear from me and asked me questions. I told him of my travel and experiences, and I could hear in his voice how happy he was to hear my stories. But we did not talk long because it was expensive, and in parting, my father advised me not to call too often because of the cost.

By my second call, my father had received the money I sent and was pleased and appreciative. Again we only spoke briefly. I called a third time during the Lunar New Year, and this time my sister answered, saying my father was lying down and not feeling well. When I called back three days later, my father was still unavailable to talk. In Chinese culture, everyone takes time off work to visit family during Lunar New Year. No matter how far they need to go, more than 300 million people still travel during the holiday to be together. *He jia tuan yuan* means "wishing every family member with you around the table, forming the full circle together." This is the greeting everyone says to one another, and it is important that all members be present. In 1985, my family's circle was broken because I was not there. I understood this. My mother had died during the holiday five years earlier, which made me anxious about my father at that time.

I did not know for several months that my father died during that holiday. My friends, the Fischers, were living in China then and had attended his funeral. Nobody told me because they knew I would have left the United States immediately, abandoning my studies and my future to see my father before he died or to honor him at his funeral. And I may never have been able to return to the U.S. Nothing was certain in those days. I have never blamed anyone for not telling me, though the grief of not being there has remained with me all my life.

When the Fischers came to Minnesota for the summer, they visited me at the university. After we hugged and chatted a bit, I asked about my father. Roland Fischer took me aside, told me of my father's death and showed me photos of him wrapped in the traditional yellow and silver cloths, with gold on top and silver below. He assured me that the service was solemn and respectful, and how it could not have been better. My father was sixty-four years old when he died, and like my mother, he was cremated. Mao had made cremation mandatory in China—against the ancient belief that you are born whole, die whole, and must be buried whole. Only then do you have peace. Many years later, I leased land in the province of my father's birth and buried my parents' ashes there, on Mount Taishan, overlooking a valley.

I was stunned by the news of my father's death in 1986. I could not eat or sleep for many days and felt overwhelming guilt for not being there with him. Instead I was far away pursuing my own, selfish goals. Care for the elderly, particularly one's parents—filial piety—is a deeply held value in Chinese culture, and one that must be demonstrated by one generation for the next. We heard this tale as children:

> A young couple lives with their seven-year-old son and the husband's mother. When the elderly mother breaks her food bowl, she is not given a new one but must continue to use the broken bowl that holds much less food. Then the child breaks his bowl, but his mother tells him not to feel bad as she will get him a new bowl. "Do not throw away my broken bowl," he tells her, "I will save it for you when you get old."

We learned this moral early—how you treat your elders is how you will be treated.

Though I will always feel the guilt of my father dying without me, I know he had goals for me and was proud that I was succeeding in life. My sisters told me he wore my uniform from the Railway Ministry every day. I was pursuing something bigger than I could comprehend, and opportunities were so rare then. Perhaps doors opened for me because my ancestors had done good things in their lives, built bridges, patched roads, made marriage matches, or gave food to the poor. This, too, is part of the culture—that the good your ancestors did will come back to you. Charity in China does not come from government-sanctioned charitable giving, because no one trusts where that money will end up. Instead, we believed that one good turn deserves another, and that goodness rubs off through the ages.

Though I grieved my father's death for months, I needed to move forward with my life in the United States, which was different from China in every way. All my exploring seemed to lead me to places I did not intend. In my first year of college, I noticed that there were public bathhouses in the city. This made me curious, since everyone I met lived in houses with multiple bathrooms and plenty of hot water at their disposal. I mentioned to my roommate that I might like to visit a public bathhouse and that I had gone to the public bathhouse in China once a week for twenty-five cents a visit. He did not know what to make of that, but discouraged me from going. He said public bathhouses were different than those in China.

Ignoring his advice, I took a bus downtown to a bathhouse. Right away I noticed that there were no women, only men. The door at the entrance was small, the place dark, and I was wary of the way those men looked at me. They did not seem like fellow bathers. I did not understand, so I left. Later David explained that these bathhouses were not about taking a bath, that there was another agenda.

My naivete on such matters tripped me up. Considering different courses I might take to broaden my education, I discovered a class in sex education. It looked like a good one-credit course, so I enrolled. I could not believe what was covered in that course! Everything was a revelation to me.

Around the same time, my roommate took a job working at the front desk of our dormitory at night, where a wide assortment of magazines was available to borrow, from *Time* and *Newsweek* to *Playboy* and *Playgirl*. I thought I should try to better understand relationships between men and women in the world, so I checked out a *Playgirl* magazine, assuming it would have photos and articles about females. I brought it to the privacy of the top bunk in my room and was beyond shocked when I opened it and saw pictures I did not want to see. Somehow word managed to leak out that I had checked out a *Playgirl* magazine, and my roommate again had to explain to me why there were images of men in a magazine called *Playgirl*. These are the things that happen when you are learning a new culture.

I was always striving to find new ways to learn English. In my second year at the university, I took a part-time evening job at the hospital, copying doctors' notes and preparing packets of needles for blood tests. It was there I met a nurse, Louann Koopmeiners, who befriended me. We went to the ballet together and out to dinner, and I thought she was wonderful.

Over the next weeks, I visited her parents in St. Cloud and went skiing with her in Wisconsin, where we shared a hotel room with twin beds. I had never skied in my life and by mistake found myself on an advanced hill going straight down, quickly gaining speed. Louann had skied down ahead of me, zigging and zagging to break her speed, but I had not learned that skill yet. I was heading straight into a hut when I decided I needed to fall on purpose to save my life! Years later I told her in jest, "I know you didn't want to date me, but you didn't have to kill me!" At the time, however, my experience with women was so limited that I assumed the trip alone together with such a level of intimacy meant something romantic was developing between us.

I had grown very fond of Louann and decided I would ask her to marry me. I invited her out to dinner, then went to a jewelry store and bought the biggest diamond I could afford, respectable though not extravagant. I chose a nice restaurant, where I went ahead of our dinner date to explain my plan to the maître d' and request that everything be perfect. Then I told the two fatherly figures in my life—Roland Fischer and André Gillet.

Both expressed concern. André asked me what made me think she would answer "yes." I told him about the things we had done together, and that it must be love for all that to happen. My own parents married on the same day they were introduced. But André was not so sure. He asked me about our physical connection, and I told him we had held hands, and that she had kissed me. Where did she kiss you, he asked. On the cheek, I said. On both cheeks. André remarked that American girls were different from Chinese girls. He thought I was jumping too far ahead. Roland Fischer thought the same. They were worried that I would be crushed if Louann said "no" and advised that I give the relationship more time.

But nobody could stop me. My intent was pure, I concluded, so I went ahead with my plan. We went to dinner, and when I proposed, she was shocked, truly shocked. She delicately explained that I was a good friend, but that marriage was different than friendship. It was a terrible night and I was crushed.

I waited two months to return the ring to the jewelry store, and when she called every week, I did not answer her calls. I felt rejected, and nobody likes feeling rejected. Then she sent me a postcard that changed my mind. She said she cared about me and was worried. She said she was not ready to be married, but she wanted to continue our friendship. I considered this. I wanted to be the kind of person who had friends like Louann Koopmeiners. I called her back, and our friendship has lasted to this day. When I married Rene, she was my wife's personal attendant. She is my older daughter Natalie's godmother, and the strong friendship we enjoy is one of a lifetime.

Around this time, I began volunteering at Minnesota International, a nonprofit organization which eventually hired me as a student program coordinator. This is where I met a fellow volunteer, an older woman named Mary McQuillan, who would also profoundly influence my life. She had been a buyer for Dayton's department store and had taken care of her ailing mother throughout her adult life. Mary's fiancé had been killed in a motorcycle accident when they were eighteen, and she had never met anyone else she wanted to marry. Still, she refused to be unhappy and was a role model of optimism.

Shortly after I met Mary, she took a three-week vacation and asked me if I would like to house-sit for her while she was away. This was another new concept. "Do I sit in your house?" I asked her. She told me I could sit in the house or lie down or do whatever I wanted. She asked me to care for her house in her absence and would pay me. When she returned, I had cleaned for her, mowed the grass, and cooked Chinese dumplings.

At the end of the meal, she suggested I move in and help around the house in exchange for room and board. Because I was still in school with free room and board, I postponed moving in with Mary. Later, when I was working at my first job and paying to rent an apartment, we discussed the idea again. I moved in, agreeing to cut her grass in the summer, shovel snow in the winter, and cook one meal a week. I got to know Mary well. She played beautiful piano and hosted holiday dinners in her small house for foreign students. She did all the preparations and paid for everything herself. Mary was an uplifting presence in my life. My parents were no longer alive, and I had not known my own grandparents. I felt secure and comforted by Mary's kind and motherly treatment.

But we did have our cultural differences. For example, I grew up with the habit of opening a window to let in fresh air. My roommate, Dave, had not appreciated my keeping our dorm room window open at night, especially in the winter, and neither did Mary. "I don't want to be heating the outdoors," she said. Upset at her comment, I threw extra money into our household fund to pay the heating bill.

I lived with Mary until I could comfortably afford to rent a two-bedroom, one bath apartment—a happy milestone in my life. At that time, I also needed a car, so Mary gladly volunteered to teach me how to drive. She took me to Hillside Cemetery to practice because, as she put it, "Everyone here is dead already." It was a good place to learn with hills and narrow roads, and we went many times. I had no experience with cars as most Americans do when they learn to drive. There were no cars in my youth, no dad driving with me in the car, none of that. As such, driving did not come easily to me. But Mary's car had a clutch, and whenever I did not know what to do, I shifted out of gear. I remember her saying, "The shift is there to help you drive, Brian, not to help you stop!"

Mary and I stayed close for the rest of her life. She always placed flowers on her mother's grave and when she could no longer drive, I did it for her. After she died, I continued the tradition. I still bring flowers to her and her mother's graves twice a year on Memorial Day and Thanksgiving. Sometimes I take my daughters and tell them, "This is where I learned to drive." To me, Grandma Mary was part of my family—the grandmother I did not have. She sat at the family table when I got married. I feel honored to have had her in my life.

I bought my first car in 1987, a beige Pontiac for $1,700.

It had cloth seats, no air-conditioning, no cassette player, and no power windows. But it was a nice car without much rust and I took great pride in it. I washed it myself until the weather became too cold and sent pictures to my sisters of me proudly standing next to it, wearing a suit. "Hey," I wrote, "I have a car!"

Lacking air-conditioning, that first car was too hot in the summer, so I decided to upgrade. I went to the Toyota dealer and chose a basic Corolla with all the conveniences. When the manager asked whether I wanted short-term or five-year financing, I told him, "I'd like to pay cash." To this day I have paid cash for everything I have ever purchased. I have never financed anything.

In America, I quickly learned the importance of individualism. From the start, I had so many choices, I sometimes found it overwhelming, and with the freedom to choose came the responsibility of those choices. I realized that nobody cared if I chose unwisely. It was up to me. This was such a strange but welcome surprise, to not be restricted or punished by others, but to claim my own choices and live with them.

The people I met reinforced the values I had learned from my parents. They were not the values of Mao, but more akin to the lessons of Confucius. My father had been schooled in the old teachings, so our family had always operated on respect and kindness. I learned from my father to demonstrate courage and respect for myself and others, as he did all his life.

> *When you are hungry, you stick out your stomach.*
> *When you are cold, you face the wind.*

During my first year at the University of Minnesota I majored in American Studies, eager to learn everything I could about the history and culture of this country. But André Gillet advised me that companies would be more interested in me if I had a Master of Business Administration (MBA), so in my second year I changed the course of my studies, which prolonged my schooling but enhanced my opportunities. The year I was preparing to graduate, I interviewed with various businesses that visited the university recruiting employees. I was offered a position in a family-owned company that manufactured a type of aeration equipment to rid the sludge from aquacultures. My job would be to market this equipment throughout Asia.

I was in the U.S. on a student visa, so before this manufacturing company could officially hire me, it had to go through a process of outreach to higher priority applicants, such as U.S. citizens or green card holders. Only if none of those applicants had the "readily available skills" could the company hire me. They interviewed fifty other applicants, most of whom had failed to notice that the job required fluent Chinese and 70 percent foreign travel. The personnel department told me that some conversations lasted ten seconds. "Do you speak Chinese?" No. Done. I obtained an H-visa, also known as a "labor certificate," which allowed me to work in the U.S., and I was excited to begin my first job in international trade.

One reason I chose to stay in the United States was for the opportunity to work in a good job that allowed me to travel back to China, and to Malaysia, Singapore, Japan, and South Korea. Another reason was the lack of opportunity in China. I had reached out to the Railway Ministry to inform them I was graduating with an MBA focusing on international business and finance, and to ask about jobs they might have available. This was 1988, when the country still did not have financial products, mortgages, or investments. The people at the Railway Ministry had no idea what an MBA was. They offered me a position in the library doing translations, which brought back memories of translating operating manuals years before, a tedious and uncreative task. The thought of doing such uninspiring work again was another reason I stayed in America.

Most importantly, my father had died. If he had needed me to care for him, I would have returned to China immediately after finishing my graduate studies. My sisters were still there, living lives that had improved little since childhood.

Even though their small houses had cold running water and sewage drains, and, due to the government's one-child policy, only three people per family, it was still a hard life. Working in the U.S., I had been able to send my sisters $100 a month, and if I stayed in the United States, I could continue to do so. The better my job, the more I could help them.

At the university, I became accustomed to not looking like most of the other students. I came from another place, spoke a different native language, and had lived an entirely different life prior to arriving in Minneapolis. Yet from the start, I met Americans I trusted not to harm me. In China, when the police took us to the station to "interview" us for learning English with Mr. Wu in eighth grade, I knew they were a threat to us. Nothing protected me from harm in China, yet in the U.S. I felt safe and secure with strangers. I avoided other Chinese students at the university. Most were state-sponsored and, as such, it was their duty to report anything they deemed "suspicious" behavior. I did not want to have to worry about what I said or did. I did not want to think about being reported. This was a unique experience because we were people with common roots and a common language. When we ate soup, we could slurp together as was our custom. But I chose not to socialize with them.

Also, I recognized the hierarchy of Chinese people in the U.S. At the top were the American Born Chinese (ABC) group. Then came the very wealthy, even second-generation wealthy. Those from Taiwan and Hong Kong were next in this hierarchy, followed by the lowest group—immigrants and students from mainland China, like me. Even during the Lunar

New Year, these groups in the hierarchy did not mix, which surprised me. I have never subscribed to such social orders. Instead I have always been drawn to people who are open and egalitarian.

Years of domination in China had resulted in an undercurrent of citizen brutality, which was another reason I was not eager to go back. People turned on one another, and why is that? Where does that inhumanity come from? The now famous Stanford Prison Experiment (1971) chose students who had tested normal to participate in a study about power and submission. Based on a coin toss, half the group were to act as prisoners and half as guards. Within a day, the students who were guards began to humiliate the prisoners, deprive them of food, and put them in compromising situations, while the students acting as prisoners became submissive and depersonalized. The actions of both groups were so startling and upsetting that the scheduled two-week experiment ceased after six days. The conclusions of the research, which are still discussed to this day, demonstrated the adverse impact of one group having too much power over another.

During the Cultural Revolution, college professors were beaten and abused by former students, many of whom actually admired them for their brilliant teaching. But that did not matter once these students had the power to dominate and were expected to be brutal on the pretext of keeping order. In China, we say, the arm can never wrestle with the leg; the leg always wins.

People forgot their humanity, and afterward, they whitewashed what happened. The Cultural Revolution's ten years of plundering and destruction are currently regarded as "searching for a better form of socialism," which is why it is being repeated in the twenty-first century. China does not discredit the forty years of Mao, nor does the country discredit its forty-year open door policy. Nobody thinks atrocities will happen until they do. There is a pro-Mao theorist in China today who never questioned the unjust things that happened to others until he was prevented from getting necessary medical treatment for his ninety-year-old mother. When she died from lack of intervention, he became outraged. In a major reversal of attitude, he now writes that the revolution is against him.

When my father was demoted because he had worked for the wrong side of the military in 1949, neighbors cut off the hair on one side of my mother's head to humiliate her. The Red Guard would not have known my father's status unless someone snitched on him. This is what happens in an authoritarian country. And so, for all these reasons and all the history, I kept my distance from other Chinese students at the university.

I have an instinct about people, something I got from my mother. Everyone liked her, but she knew which neighbors to bring into her confidence and which ones to keep at a polite distance. I, too, have always sensed who will be a trustworthy friend. Living in an inherited country, I have known the invisible fences that separate me from others, boundaries I know not to cross. At times I may have misread cultural cues, but I have understood who I can bring into my confidence. And I have known warm-hearted and kind people who have been my friends throughout the years.

I chose to live and work in the United States. I could have gone to Canada, Australia, or New Zealand, as I would have had enough immigration points with my degree and language skills. But I stayed here. I left my father and my sisters behind in China, at least for a time, and a few close friends from school. But what else did I lose?

I lost the government's control over my own destiny and my food insecurity and the constant fear of what would happen next. I lost an environment that allowed no options whatsoever. Families could not have the children they wanted or move to a different city. Farmers could not even grow their own crops. When I graduated from college and taught for two years, I could not create my own curriculum, could not choose a textbook or a lesson or improvise anything, because it all had been decided by others for me. I left behind the feeling of being a recording machine, an echo machine.

It is liberating to lose such things.

And what did I gain? I gained a chance to make my own choices, to take responsibility for those choices, change my mind or change my direction. I switched from American Studies to an MBA and left my first job to work for another without needing anyone's approval. I can live anywhere I want—move to Florida or Texas or any other city or go work on a farm again if I want. Here you choose the person you want to marry and have as many children as you want and do whatever you want, as long as you are not harming others. You make your own decisions and bear the consequences.

Can you imagine not having that?

Years later when my sisters arrived in this country, they did not have the language skills to get good jobs. One of my sisters washed dishes in her first months here, then learned enough English to bus dishes, then moved up to better positions. My sisters took any shift they could and accepted difficult conditions because they understood that eventually it would get better. They had the freedom to make life better for themselves. It was possible to leave behind a 120-square foot, one-room house without a bathroom in Tianjin and progress, little by little, to owning a 2,000-square foot home with a bathroom for everyone who lived there.

What happens is on your own shoulders.

That is the life I chose.

CHAPTER IX

FINDING LOVE
MINNEAPOLIS, MINNESOTA

1994 – 2003

I didn't get seriously interested in dating again until I had completed my MBA and felt secure in my entrepreneurial work. But searching for the right person in life can raise such self-doubts, something I had never experienced before. I had stayed in touch with my colleagues from the Railway Ministry, all of whom had done well in life, had been frequently promoted in their careers, and were content with their lives in China. In one conversation, an old friend asked how many children I had. I replied that I had no children because I was not yet married. He was shocked. Given my education and professional status, he believed I should have any number of women wishing to marry me. Come to China, my friends told me, and we will introduce you to kind and beautiful women from good families.

So I went to China in search of a wife.

In certain periods of Chinese history, scouts ventured out into the countryside to find beautiful women for the nobles to marry. In a modern sense, this is what my friends did for me. I used a railway pass to ride in the sleeper car of the train through many provinces, where I met eight lovely and refined women. In one week, I traveled 3,000 miles from Harbin in the north, where the women tend to have the beauty of Russians, to Port Arthur in Dalian and Tianjin, then Qingdao, where the influence is German. I went all the way south to Chengdu, where the water supposedly gives people perfect complexions, and then on to Hangzhou, where the explorer Marco Polo claimed to have seen the most beautiful women in the world.

At the end of the week, after not meeting anyone I wanted to marry, I made my plans to return to the United States. All the women I met and talked with were the daughters of professors or officials. They were educated and well-mannered, and their families were at a high level in the Chinese socioeconomic hierarchy. During feudal times, the country operated on a system of seven levels. Everyone knew your level of importance by the height of your door threshold. People were executed for having a higher threshold than their level allowed. The Communists adopted and modified that system in their own way, with perks for each level. Mao and his group were level one. Nobody was higher than they were. The lowest level was twenty-four. Intermediate levels depended on education and position. When you made it to level thirteen, you were considered high ranking and would be given a chauffeur or car. As a college graduate, I automatically advanced to level twenty-two. But on the farm, I was at the lowest level, even lower than a vegetable street vendor.

I concluded that all the women I had met were at higher levels than I was. I could not help but think that if I were still on the farm, if I had not been accepted into college and were not in possession of a green card, none of them would have been attainable. China—and these young women—continued to function in a world of rigid divisions between those who were poor, as my family had been, and those who enjoyed the privileges these women had known. They were not changed. But I was changed. More importantly, I had a romanticized view. I wanted to fall in love first, then get married, not get married and hope to fall in love later. For those reasons, I returned home alone.

I never felt comfortable with the idea of employing dating services, and instead met various women through people I knew. Sometimes they were more interested in me than I was in them. Sometimes I was more interested in them than they were in me. I came to learn that the three worst words in dating are, "Let's be friends." I also did not like to hear, "You're a wonderful man who will make a wonderful father someday"—just not with me.

Because I was consulting on importing and exporting at that time, I was a member of the International Trade Association. At one of the organization's potluck dinners, a Japanese friend of mine introduced me to Irene Rafferty, a former senior buyer at Target Stores, Inc. who was working as a manufacturer's representative for a Taiwanese company. Irene was impressed with the pot stickers I had brought to the party, and over the next six months, we developed a professional and personal connection. She frequently mentioned that I had to meet her friend Rene Wyman because she thought we would have a lot in common. I later learned she told Rene the same thing. One day in April 1995, Irene asked me to stop by her office at ten in the morning to show her some candle samples. I was dressed professionally in a suit and tie, arrived on time, and showed her the line of candles she was interested in purchasing. As I stood up to leave, she initiated another conversation. "Stay and visit awhile," she said.

Shortly after that, a very attractive woman entered Irene's office, surprised to see me there. Ensuring that our meetings would overlap, Irene had scheduled a meeting with Rene at ten thirty a.m. to discuss her MBA project. That was it for me. I asked Irene for Rene's phone number, but Irene told me she would have to check with her first. I heard back by the end of the day and called Rene that same evening. "Irene said you might call," she said, and we ended up talking for two hours.

Because she was in school and I was traveling, it took two weeks to schedule our first date, which was at a nice restaurant in the IDS Tower downtown Minneapolis. We continued to get to know each another and planned a second date soon after. I had season tickets to a concert at the Minnesota Orchestra the following weekend, so I cooked dinner at her house, then we went to the concert. During intermission, I introduced her to friends, four couples who had season tickets to the same concerts. Though she has always believed it was a setup so they could check her out, I viewed it as an opportunity to introduce someone I was dating to friends who had known me for years. A week later we went out to dinner again, then we visited Grandma Mary, my gatekeeper, who liked Rene immediately.

Over the years I had developed a "List of Attributes for Brian Chang's Wife." The first item on my list was education, followed by cultured, kind, soft-spoken, and well-mannered. I was impressed that she was well-educated, and I preferred a woman who enjoyed traveling. And there were bonuses: Rene had blond hair, and she grew up in St. Paul in a large, extended Irish Catholic family. I felt warmly welcomed into that family and even came to call her mother "Mom." Rene was the woman of my dreams!

After only three dates, I was confident that we were right for one another, and I knew I would propose. Without warning or expectation, I found the love of my life. She was beautiful, hard-working, intelligent, and we could talk for hours. I felt something I had not felt before, validating my wisdom to wait for love. We met in April and I proposed in August.

The proposal was exceptionally romantic. My good friend Jesse Parker and his wife, Amy, owned a cottage in Martha's Vineyard, where they spent time in the summer, with a guest cottage next door. They told me, "Come to Boston and we'll give you the guest cottage on the water." This was such a generous offer. Rene and I flew to Boston, spent the night with the Parkers, then went with them and their two children to the island.

On our engagement day, Jesse and Amy had recommended a special restaurant, and said that they would have a surprise waiting when we returned from dinner. I had selected a good-sized diamond ring with the help of my friend, Louann, who accompanied me to three different jewelers to find the perfect ring. At the restaurant, I got down on one knee to propose and offered Rene the ring, while "popping the question." When Rene and I returned to their cottage, holding hands and the engagement ring on her finger, the Parkers served cake and champagne to celebrate. They went out of their way to make our evening as romantic as possible. It was a wonderful engagement.

We had hoped to have our wedding the following June, but Colonial Church, where I had been a member for years, was booked for the entire month. We asked about May. They were booked for May as well. Rene would have been happy to be married in April, but April is the fourth month of the year, and in Mandarin, the number four and death have very similar pronunciations. It is considered bad luck to get married in the "death" month of April. Most Chinese hotels do not even have a fourth floor. So we agreed on the month of March, specifically March 16th, which was an even day on both the Gregorian and Lunar calendars. Rene was worried about the weather at that time of year, yet it turned out to be a beautiful spring day with unseasonably warm temperatures. There was a brief sprinkle of rain before the sun came out, but precipitation on your wedding day is considered good luck.

We were married at Colonial Church and held the reception at Hunan Garden Restaurant in downtown St. Paul, which closed for the evening to accommodate our group of 150 family and friends. I added some items to the menu and vetoed the cream cheese wontons, though I did compromise on the fortune cookies! Because our wedding was the day before St. Patrick's Day, downtown St. Paul was filled with revelers attending the parade and celebrating. I remember passersby making faces at us through the window, and a few even came in to congratulate us.

When Rene and I flew to Tianjin, China to host a reception before our U.S. wedding, we all traveled to the U.S. Embassy in Beijing and—miraculously—we were able to secure visas for all three sisters to travel from China to attend our U.S. wedding. Friends also flew in from around the country to celebrate with us. Our family and friends helped make it a magical day!

To me love is a flower that is nurtured over time. It continues to grow and flourish, it changes and evolves with the challenges of life. I tried so long and so hard to find someone—and then I met Rene.

We were eager to start a family. After a series of reproductive health challenges over the next several years, we decided to consider adoption. My work at that time took me to China frequently. I had facilitated a joint venture between a local Chinese company and an American one to establish a pipeline construction company in Tai'an, a town of 5-1/2 million people in Shandong province. As a result of this project, I had many contacts there. When one of my friends in Tai'an learned of our interest in adoption, he told me an infant girl had become available at their local Social Welfare Services Facility. We immediately made arrangements to fly to China to meet her, bringing baby clothes and supplies, full of anticipation and excitement.

As soon as we arrived at the facility, in August 2001, Rene locked eyes with the adorable, tiny baby who reached out for her and did not even cry when Rene held her. Rene never wanted to put her down ever again. Because Chinese law did not permit adoption of infants under six months old, we had to wait. But we stayed there, and Rene visited her every day.

As a gesture of gratitude, I thought it appropriate to make a donation to the facility where we found our daughter. The summer had been hot, and because the children's rooms lacked air-conditioning, I donated $5,000 to purchase twenty room air conditioners for the facility. We held an official ceremony, but officials told me that they could not specify exactly how the donation was spent. To this day, I am not sure if the air conditioners were ever purchased. Due to this contribution and my status as the first American investor in Tai'an, I was made an honorary citizen and granted a key to the city.

We brought our daughter, Natalie Mary Chang, home on a beautiful October day in 2001. Our neighbors had hung a large banner in front of our house in Minneapolis that read,

"Welcome Home, Baby Natalie." Rene chose her first name, and I chose Mary after Grandma Mary, who had died earlier that year. After overcoming reproductive health obstacles, we were thrilled when our second beautiful daughter, Melanie, was born two years later in December of 2003, just in time for a tax deduction! Our two "miracle" children were gifts from Heaven.

Melanie, Rene, Natalie, Brian, 2004

Natalie, Brian, Rene, Melanie, 2022

Part Two:
Opportunity in the United States

CHAPTER X

ADVENTURES IN INTERNATIONAL BUSINESS
MINNEAPOLIS AND CHINA

1988 – 2005

I have spent my professional life doing business with China and helping companies, both large and small, work effectively with China. My first job brought me into the world of agricultural business. The family-owned company had originally hoped to sell their aeration products to golf courses in China, but there were very few golf courses in China at that time. Instead, we discovered our niche in aquatic agriculture, also known as fish farms. This job revealed how little American companies understood about operating internationally. Business plans were built on assumptions that, in the end, had very little to do with reality—such as golf courses in China during the 1980s.

For years, China has appeared to be an enormous market for any number and types of goods or services. American companies only considered the number of people in a country the size of China and believed they would strike gold selling even simple products—like toothbrushes, for example. They projected that if only half the people in China bought a toothbrush, it would produce a small fortune with very little overhead. The potential seemed unlimited. But what was the primary assumption in this projection? That Chinese people would want to brush their teeth and be able to do so. The problem for the toothbrush manufacturers was that most Chinese people did not have running water, let alone the income to purchase toothpaste. How far did rural people have to walk to a creek or source of running water to brush their teeth? The marketers failed to understand the culture or day-to-day living situations. They had no grasp on how little incentive there was for the Chinese to use toothbrushes.

The company I worked for was small and had hired me to help them navigate the cultural issues of doing business in Asia. They heeded my input, and in return, I learned the operations of a small-sized company. The owner had been a Navy captain in World War II and had a special interest in China. His son did not share the same interest, so when the father died, I was ready to move on and try something new. I had worked there almost three years.

I applied for a position in the finance department of Cargill, Inc., a global agricultural conglomerate based in the Twin Cities. The interviews took a full day, beginning with the highest-ranking executive in the Asia division, then with a product-line president, and finally with mid- and peer-level staff who would be my immediate supervisors. I was hired and very proud to be working for a company of that size and stature.

Even though I reported to the finance department, my training began with six months working as a grain trader, buying, and selling corn, barley, and soybeans, and assessing the risk of transactions based on the geography, the season, and the economic efficiencies of the trade. I was surprised to be granted this much freedom to make my own business

decisions so early on, even though I was limited by dollar amount. The company empowered its employees to buy and sell commodities from all over the world. At the end of the week, I would tally my gains and losses. I found that it was acceptable to make mistakes but repeating them was not. This was an extraordinary training experience.

Working as a grain trader required visiting farms in North and South Dakota, as well as Minnesota. Some of the farmers would take one look at me and say, "The company doesn't send out people like you very often." I understood what that meant. My answer to them was, "At times they have to send someone really special." This humor would break the ice with most farmers, but others clearly took me for an outsider.

I talked to the farmers about my own experiences working on a farm in China. Fertilizer there, I would tell them, is very close to nature. In fact, we made our own! The contrasts between farming as I knew it and the farms I encountered in my Cargill job were stark. On farms like the one I worked on in the Chinese countryside, hundreds of people labored with almost no equipment. We dried and sifted the grains by hand. The farms I visited in the U.S. tended to be owned by one family who ran them with all kinds of equipment—combines and large tractors, and stainless-steel silos for storage. That was the difference. China was all about labor. In America, it was modern equipment and technology. But my experience on the village farm enabled me to understand harvests and fertilizers and all the steps involved to prepare grain for market.

The six months I spent doing trading futures was an invaluable eduction on how to manage risk. I have applied that knowledge to every job I have had since then.

As a finance employee with Chinese language skills, I was part of a corporate team that went to Shanghai to set up a joint venture cotton and silk factory. The local company had sixty little pickup trucks and 120 drivers, but my Cargill managers had decided to replace all of them with two large semi-trucks. I did not learn this until we were in China at the joint venture meeting. I was a lower-level employee, but felt I had to explain to the executive in charge why this approach would not work. Large semi-trucks would not fit on the streets, would not be able to make tight turns, and would not be able to cross city bridges without collapsing them. Moreover, we could get rid of the drivers, but they would still be on the payroll because they were state employees. My input came as a surprise to the executive team. But I was surprised that they would make such a major commitment without conducting sufficient due diligence to understand the obstacles they were facing. Worse, this all occurred during the commitment reveal meeting to finalize the deal. It was awkward that so many stakeholders were present, but I left the meeting in good conscience, knowing I had prevented an expensive error. This is an example of what was happening to large companies in the early days of conducting business with China.

Later my team worked on another joint venture to produce edible oil in partnership with a cotton seed extraction plant in Shandong Province, which is a key cotton-producing area of China. The plan was to construct the factory ten miles from the cotton fields in the city of Jinan for easy transport between the fields and the factory. But my team did not know or understand that the only road between the factory site and the city was unpaved and made of dirt, passable only by donkey carts. My question was: how many donkey carts would be needed to transport that cotton?

I came to understand how companies that wanted to do business in China assumed conditions like stable infrastructure with passable roads and sturdy bridges. But in China then and in China now, nothing can be taken for granted. Moreover, any government entity can decide to question what you are doing and get in your way. The Chinese Environmental Protection Agency (EPA) actively puts up obstacles for businesses, and not necessarily over environmental concerns. The fire department can show up any time on any given day to shut down your entire enterprise for some random "safety inspection." Anything can happen. Your water might be shut off, deliveries prohibited, or workers not provided to unload your trucks or ships in the harbor.

Your imagination is never vivid enough to project the cost of conducting business in China until you are actually there doing business. That is what I learned. Consider the basic Chinese system for heating buildings. The winter season is defined as the period between November 15 and March 15, when the heat is turned on everywhere north of the Yangtze River. But China is an enormous country with thousands of miles north to south. If you live near Siberia or operate a business anywhere in the north, it is still very cold on March 16, with temperatures well below freezing. And there is nowhere to go with your complaints.

In the world of Chinese business just because something works today does not mean it will work tomorrow. Or it may work in Shanghai, but not necessarily in Beijing. Those who succeed in doing business in China must be quick to adapt and change. In my experience, two things that commonly go wrong for foreign businesses are running out of cash and running out of patience. Either way they end up running from China.

I had a friend from Singapore who set up a couple of quality fast food restaurants in China. He spoke perfect Chinese, but he had lived in a capitalist country with the reasonable expectations of capitalism. He could not foresee that every public official he encountered would want to eat at his restaurants for free. He never imagined such a lack of pride could exist.

He ended up routinely serving complimentary meals to the police and fire department, the tax department, and all their relatives. If any of these people were not satisfied with their treatment, my friend found himself facing obstacles like the "No Loading" sign in front of his business or random sanitation inspections or fines for dirty water. Finally he gave up and went home. He wrote off his losses and did not even bother to pack.

During the time I worked for Cargill and before that, I was also volunteering at the Minnesota International Center, where I had been a translator as a student. That was in the late 1980s, early 1990s, when China had begun to expand its business dealings to the United States, Japan, and other countries. Deng Xiaoping, president from 1978 to 1989, had a broad view of what China could be. Large corporations in Minnesota such as 3M, General Mills, and Medtronic were interested in its huge untapped market and rushed to set up offices in Chinese cities, buying from and selling to China, and organizing joint ventures to demonstrate their presence as an integral part of their competitive strategies. To help them, the International Center offered one-day China Practicums, during which I taught a two-hour course.

I developed a menu of cultural areas for this course that I believed American businesses needed to consider, covering the geography of China, where more than fifty-five different nationalities live (including Laotians, Koreans, Russians, Tibetans, Burmese, etc.). Many of these nationalities do not look like "Han" Chinese, who are the largest ethnic group in China and in the world. I explained how the political system works from top to bottom and talked about the general conditions of people living in China. Many of the people attending these classes were veteran businesspeople. In my course, they learned a few basic Chinese words, how to use chopsticks, and how to count. My short class also presented cultural differences surrounding food and dining, including exotic ingredients and noisy eating habits. I thought it important for people to understand the subtle differences in communication, such as how Chinese avoid making direct eye contact, shake hands lightly, and never slap shoulders or backs or touch others during their business dealings, especially those of the opposite sex. It was even important to understand that people smoked everywhere without restrictions, like in elevators, and how it was not considered offensive in China.

After my classes there were always many questions. I saw the need for further training, consulting and translating to foster business deals in China, but as the employee of Cargill, I did not offer any of these services to the corporate representatives in my classes. Two years passed. At Cargill, employees who desired to climb the management hierarchy tended to physically move every two years or so, but as I neared that two-year mark, I realized I did not want to leave the Twin Cities. I also realized I did not require—or even crave—the security that comes with working long-term for one company.

To me living and working in the United States was more than enough security. By then I had seen how hard work and dedication paved the way to success. Businesspeople taking my course had already asked me for help, so I believed I could go out on my own and make it work. I did not know everything, but I knew that my English language skills were better than most Chinese, and that my Chinese language skills were better than almost any American.

This country is a place for rebellious spirits. The sky is the limit and you can use your energy, follow your dream, and make things happen.

I decided to start a business helping others conduct trade with China.

I found it easy to start a business in the United States. In China, there are many rules, restrictions, and bureaucratic hurdles. For one thing, in China you cannot use geography in naming your enterprise unless you are state-owned, such as China Petroleum, which is a national level state conglomerate. Sichuan, a province in southwest China known for its spicy cuisine, has Sichuan Municipal Investment, a provincial level state-owned enterprise. Tai'an, a prefecture level city, has the Tai'an Gondola Company. Prefecture level cities rank below a province but above a county. Such a name would indicate that the company is state-owned at the prefecture level. Small, private businesses can be named only for what they do or where they are, and the liability of a private company is limited to the amount of money registered and deposited in the bank. Only then does the business get a company seal and the required permits from the bank, the commerce industry bureaus, and the local government, which then allow accounts payables, receivables, and open bidding.

If these rules were not in place, companies could set

themselves up without capital, take customers' money, then close down, which was not uncommon. A barber shop, for example, might open and sell discount cards for future haircuts if customers paid in advance. People would buy the card, the barbershop would close, and the owner would walk away with the money.

Many people in China have experienced scams like that, including me. A shoe-shine franchise in Tianjin sold cards to prepay for twenty shines at a 75 percent discount. The franchise operated for a few months, then shut down. People had useless cards and no place to get their shoes shined—and nobody knew what happened to the franchise owner. The restrictions were in place to prevent small companies from unscrupulous practices. However, this good intention was abused, too. Government officials and even low-level clerks abused their power or position to demand favors and advantages. Depending on the scale of the favor, the price of obtaining a permit could be cash, a fancy car, a watch, or high-end designer suit.

Chinese people are known for being ingenious. To circumvent regulations, small architecture firms with little or no design training would find a way to use the license of a larger company with a massive amount of registered capital through bribery. People have died as a result of this type of fraud. Buildings and bridges have collapsed because designers were not qualified to do the work. When one bridge collapsed before its opening, the builders just put up a barrier to hide the disaster—if you do not see it, it is not there.

The underlying assumption in China is that, given an opportunity, everyone will cheat, so rules are enforced to ensure that people do not. The American system assumes people will follow rules. But if you do cheat, you are criminally liable and pay the consequences; the punitive damage will have a greater impact than any money that might have been made. Businesspeople in the U.S. have a choice, but the consequences are steep. In China, there is no choice because the system assumes unethical behavior by design. I started my own business fully aware of the ethics component—or potential lack thereof—in business dealings.

My initial consulting opportunity was with 3M, one of the first businesses to operate in China. Their presence continued to grow over the years, which meant that many of the company's managers were sent to work in China. The man whose family I stayed with during my first Christmas in the U.S. worked in finance for 3M. He had been a lawyer who was shrewd at recognizing business efforts that might grow into something big. He invited me to a function where I met the human resource executive in charge of assigning employees to China. I was asked to talk about culture and customs to a director-level manager who was soon to be stationed in Shanghai. But what started as a two-hour consultation became a broader contract when the director realized I had business experience and could consult with him on concerns like paying employees and giving raises.

Through word-of-mouth my consulting and translating work continued. I had the ability to advise businesspeople on cultural differences and to help resolve situations involving

cultural misunderstandings. At one point, I was hired by a die set company to translate and consult on a Chinese deal. The managers of the company were not refined men. During a conversation with the Chinese company executive, the American manager told a crude joke which he expected me to translate so we could all have a laugh together. Translating that joke was impossible. It would have ended the deal right then and there. So, in Chinese, I said to the executive, "My colleague here just told a joke that is too difficult for me to translate. But when I am done talking, please laugh to indulge him, and we will continue with the negotiations." The Chinese executive laughed, the American was happy, and we moved forward.

I had worked on my own for almost five years when a new opportunity arose. My long-time friend Jesse Parker was hired by Soft Bank in Boston, which had invested sixteen million dollars in the Chinese Internet company, Alibaba. Jesse was the vice president in charge of expansion into China, and he sought my help. For the first six months I was a consultant, and when the company made me an offer too good to refuse, I went to work as Director of Soft Bank Greater China, which included Hong Kong, Macau, and Taiwan. Companies approached us for initial public offerings, and after they made their presentations, it was my job to either accept or decline the offer. I did not just analyze each situation, but also made a judgment. If I did not trust a company, I was given an opportunity to present my case.

When the dot com bubble burst in 2000, my division was "right sized" to nonexistence, but I was not worried. There were always opportunities, and the next one came as a surprise. In my early years in the United States, I cooked and taught cooking as a way to make friends and to contribute to charitable events. Just after I left Soft Bank Greater China, I donated Chinese dinners, which I would cook in the winning bidder's home to raise money for the International Center, where I had worked many years before. One of these dinners was hosted by the vice chairman of Alliance Capital. We talked, first about my food and then about our work, and he invited me to meet with him at his office to continue our conversation. Alliance was interested in investing in China. They offered me a position as a large cap analyst reviewing companies capitalized at ten billion or more. This was something different for me, but the fundamental business questions were

the same: was a product superior, what was the market share, what would it look like in five years, and so on. I found the job mentally stimulating and rewarding. But after Enron went bankrupt in 2003, Alliance lost $350 million in stocks. Shares worth forty dollars sold for twenty-eight dollars, and the vice chairman who hired me left the company.

In 2004, I was back on my own. I found that my experiences working for Soft Bank and Alliance were very much like being an independent consultant because I had the autonomy and freedom to make high-level, impactful business decisions. In all cases, I functioned as an entrepreneur initiating projects and strategies—I did not wait for instructions or manuals to guide me. I believe this entrepreneurial attribute has made me successful, as well as the businesses I have worked with throughout the years. I cannot help but think that my entrepreneurial instincts and skills are a reaction to all the restrictions I experienced in China. When I lived on the farm, I was told what to do every day. Even after I received my degree and was teaching, I was told what to teach and when and how. All those years, someone else gave me directions, telling me they were the best directions, even when I knew they were not. I was always ready to think for myself and to carve my own path. Then, too, I was a product of the Class of 1977, whose graduates branched out all over the world to break new ground in a variety of fields.

Throughout the years, traveling back and forth to China, I witnessed constant change and opportunities that had not existed in my youth. Enterprises of the late '90s and early 2000s would have been impossible dreams just decades earlier. Soon after I returned to consulting, I became involved in building what is now the Radisson Hotel in Tianjin. It started out as a twenty-three-story, 300,000-square-foot structure built by a government business. Before it could be finished, China issued a new directive prohibiting any government entity from operating hotels. This was another of those sudden moves by the central government to restrict something they thought might be benefiting too many people or the wrong people.

Under this directive, hotels were passed to state-owned businesses, and the unfinished hotel in Tianjin then became the problem of the general manager for real estate, who happened to be our family's neighbor and a good friend of my father. He helped my sisters after I left China and my parents passed away, and I was so grateful to him, I stayed in touch throughout the years, meeting him for dinner whenever I was back in town. I operated on my father's belief that if you are given a drop of water when you are thirsty, you return with a fountain. This is why I maintain lifelong connections and friendships. I do not take kindness lightly.

In one of our conversations, this friend and neighbor asked me if I knew any Americans who could finish the hotel, and I immediately thought of an architect and friend named Mike Lyner, a brother-in-law of the family I lived with when I first arrived. Mike was a principal and architect at RSP Architects, a Minneapolis-based company that was interested in expanding internationally.

Mike and I discussed this opportunity with the owner of his firm, Dave Norback, and he immediately said, "Let's go." Within eight weeks we had completed all of the paperwork and were on our way to China. Three men from RSP and I flew into Beijing and out of Shanghai to Tianjin to give the team a feeling for the country. My Chinese contacts liked the contingent from RSP Architects, who were intelligent and courteous. They hired them on the spot to finish the hotel.

Soon we were presented with the cultural issues, starting with titles used to designate who was who. In China, an architect is someone who does drawings and nothing more. An architect has no leadership on any project, zero. In China, it is the engineers who make decisions and lead projects. We needed to clarify that difference. The next issue was the design model. As creative, intelligent professionals, RSP wanted to develop an elaborate model to present to the Chinese. I needed to explain that no matter how wonderful their design was, they should expect numerous recommended changes because many levels of government would need to approve the design, and every level would add a change just to demonstrate their intelligence. Each person at each level would want his own idea incorporated into the design. "Show them pictures," I said. "Let them look at lots of designs and choose the elements they want."

It is very difficult for a creative company to accept that approach, but the Chinese are not necessarily interested in originality; it is not part of the culture. If you travel in China you may see some unique structures, but you will also see many renditions of the White House, the Empire State Building, the Eiffel Tower, the Leaning Tower of Pisa, and the Washington Monument. Forget about originality. RSP heeded my suggestion, creating a beautiful, and ultimately unique, design that looked modern and Western, with a lotus flower design element at the top of the hotel to reflect Chinese culture.

The Chinese then asked for help finding an American company to operate the hotel. After speaking with several U.S. hotel companies, Radisson Hotels—owned and operated by Carlson Company—made the best offer. Their Asia division president thought Tianjin, which was a port city with easy access, would be an ideal location for them, so we proceeded with the joint venture. Sheraton and Hyatt also expressed interest, but I favored the idea of working with a Minnesota-based company.

Again, we had cultural issues to work through, the primary one being the heating and cooling system. Chinese-run hotels at that time had only two pipes running into the building, one for cool air in the summer and another for hot air in the winter. When I first brought Dave Norback to China, it was winter, and his room was uncomfortably hot. He was having trouble adjusting the thermostat on the wall, so I called for maintenance to help. I will never forget it. The maintenance man showed up at the door in his blue uniform with an insignia on the pocket, carrying a huge bag of tools. When he asked, "What's the problem?" I replied that the room was too hot. "Easy to fix," he said, as he set down his tools and opened the window. We were speechless! "What about the thermostat?" I asked. "That? It's for decoration." Because it was an American-operated hotel, there were people available at night to answer the phones and send help. In Chinese-managed hotels at the time, the lights went off when it was time to sleep. You sleep and they sleep.

I tell this story to indicate the status quo for heating and cooling in China at the time the Radisson executive negotiated the Tianjin project. Radisson Hotels have standards. Every hotel needed year-round heating and air-conditioning. That meant four pipes would need to go into the hotel, which was a problem for the Chinese. I translated back and forth as the Chinese argued, why would someone need cold air in January or hot air in July and why should they have that choice anyway? The decision had already been made for them to keep the rooms warm in cold weather and cool in hot weather. In China the heat goes on November 15, regardless of the outside temperature. And on March 15, the heat is turned off no matter what. The government decides because this was the way they were used to doing things. The argument went on for two days.

Finally, I convinced them that not adding the two extra pipes was a deal-breaker, and that if the Asia President from Carlson Company, the highest-ranking executive on this project, said "no,"¹ the deal was off. The Chinese wanted this American hotel in Tianjin, a city of about 10 million people, which, at that time, only had Hyatt, Sheraton, and Renaissance Hotels. They finally relented and the Radisson Hotel was constructed with the four-pipe HVAC system.

Radisson Hotels are five-star enterprises. To qualify, four fixtures are required in every bathroom: a shower, a bathtub, a sink, and a toilet. Having all four fixtures in each hotel room takes up more space and adds to the cost, but Radisson was not interested in a three-star hotel. A five-star hotel also required an elevator that moved quickly, keeping customers waiting only a maximum of thirty seconds, with a separate service elevator, a completely foreign concept to our Chinese partners. Why two elevators? I had to explain that all American hotels have a separate elevator for hauling dirty laundry and room service trays, which customers do not want to see or smell in the elevator. For the Chinese, this was truly a learning process.

Working with the Chinese was also a steep learning curve for one member of the RSP team who did not observe the all-important cultural nuances involved with international business communication. His behavior offers lessons for what not to do when pursuing business in China. He was a very talented man, but he was not the person with seniority—neither by title nor age—and that is critical in China. He did not pick up on the need to defer to the senior person. In Chinese culture, a person who is not in charge does not ask to be served first, or pull out pictures of his children to show out of turn. I needed to explain the hierarchy to him—that the host always sits in the middle of the table facing the door with the official next in line to his right. Dinner is served according to pecking order, not because someone calls out, "Serve me first." The rules are unspoken, but they are easily observed. Open your eyes, I tell people when we travel together. See how things are done.

This man and I took one trip to Tianjin without other RSP staff, and at the end of the long day, he complained that he was too tired to go to dinner. That, too, was unacceptable and disrespectful. Business not only extends to mealtime, but it may be even more important than the meetings. Maybe you have approval for the project today, but if you do not show up at dinner, you may not have approval tomorrow. Dinner and entertainment are part of the work, part of making the deal.

This representative from RSP and I traveled to China together ten times, and it never got any better. My Tianjin contact commented that this man "must be very talented." And it was not meant as a compliment. When the Chinese say, "You must be very talented," it means, "You must be talented to be here because you are not good at anything else." It can also be translated as, "We cannot fire you—yet!" My Tianjin contact tried to give the American tips on how to fit in more appropriately, but it never worked. Privately, he told me, "He's only good for a toothpick," meaning all the best wood is used for better things, and this wood is only good for a toothpick!

It is not that difficult to do the right thing to respect another culture. If you wait twenty seconds to see what others are doing, you understand. Why is nobody sitting down? Maybe it is because the host is not sitting down. Fitting into another culture is a matter of paying attention and showing respect.

A visitor can never expect their hosts to adapt to them.
In our global society, there is much to learn, always, and much to gain.

CHAPTER XI

MOVING TO CHINA AND LESSONS LEARNED
TIANJIN AND BEIJING

2006 – 2017

At the time of the Radisson Hotel project in Tianjin, RSP began to consider expanding internationally. We discussed the idea of my being stationed in China as the on-site general manager using my local network to secure further projects, but by this time, I had been married for nearly a decade and had young children. Constant travel meant that I was away more than I wanted to be.

When our daughter Natalie was old enough to speak, I began teaching her Chinese because it was important to me that my daughters speak my native language. But this would be a challenge because we all spoke English to each other at home. The opportunity to work for RSP in China meant that my daughters could go to school where everyone spoke Chinese, and as young girls, they would learn to speak Mandarin as a normal part of their lives.

In 2006, after two years of negotiating with RSP and traveling thousands of miles back and forth to China, I accepted the position as the company's chief representative and general manager in China and moved with my family to Tianjin. It was the best way to manage continuing projects, the impromptu meetings, and the many local decisions and relationships. I was there to run a successful business, and ran it as if it were my own, maintaining my contacts and spending money as wisely as if it were my own.

Rene grew up in St. Paul, Minnesota, and Tianjin was far away from her family and friends in Minnesota, so she had many concerns. She agreed to consider a move to China as long as we reassessed after two years, and I promised that we would return to the U.S. if she was not happy. We did not sell our house in Minneapolis just in case. But I was certain she would be so charmed by our life in China, she would choose to stay.

We arrived in Tianjin in October 2006 and enrolled Natalie and Melanie in kindergarten classes at Nankai University, the most prestigious university in Tianjin, and later Rene got a job teaching conversational English and International Negotiations courses at Tianjin Normal University and Foreign Language School. We started out living at the Sheraton Hotel, but Rene missed having a place to call home, so we settled into a lovely 1,500-square foot apartment in a high-rise for expatriates, where she had housekeeping help and a part-time driver.

I felt happy to be back. There is a story about a young Chinese fellow who is poor and without a future. He leaves his village for many years then returns after he becomes successful. His hair is white, he wears nice clothes, and speaks excellent Mandarin. Although my hair was not white yet, I was returning a successful businessman, managing the subsidiary of an American company, with a beautiful wife and two lovely daughters. While we lived at the Sheraton, old friends came to visit, somewhat in awe of the luxurious rooms and glass elevator. Some had never even been in a hotel before. I had worked hard, taken many risks, and could not help but feel proud. My life in no way resembled what it was when I was a child. In fact, the entire neighborhood where I grew up had been demolished and replaced with apartment buildings and a shopping mall. New World Development out of Hong Kong had purchased ten square miles of land where I used to live, paid people to leave, then rebuilt the whole area. Even my school had been torn down.

Before I left for China, my oldest sister told me not to trust the locals with RSP's money. "You've been an American for too long, you're naive," she told me. "Don't let them control the purse." "Okay," I answered, then asked, "Do you want to come and do it for me?" She said she would think about it, and within hours she called to tell me she would. She left her family, who lived in the United States by then, and stayed in China for two years to help me.

There were many authorizations required to do business in China, including more than twenty different stamps from various departments such as commerce, foreign investment, foreign currency control, personnel, and tax audit, as well as the union, the bank, and quality control. Nobody gave me a list and told me to come back with all these approvals. Instead I could only get one approval at a time, as they could not give the next one until I presented the one before that first. As such, the tedious process took forever. And with each trip to a different government office, I brought a small gift—candies or trinkets of some kind—to offer to the low-level employee working with me. That is how the system operates.

RSP did well in Tianjin. Dave Norback, the chairman, traveled there frequently to make presentations. Dave was in his late fifties then, polished and engaging, quick-witted, and able to communicate and connect without the benefit of knowing much of the language. In response, the Chinese were open and eager. They found the Western designs refreshing and innovative, even avant-garde. Dave and I worked well together and secured many projects.

Rene, however, struggled with Tianjin's less cosmopolitan culture. It was not as international as Shanghai or Beijing, and she missed common products like peanut butter, pasta, cheese, and breakfast cereal. In addition, my work demanded many evening meetings entertaining clients, and I found myself away from home more than I wanted to be. After one year, we decided to move to Beijing, where more resources were available for expats, and we found an apartment close to my longtime friends Adam and Judy Pillsbury. Rene took a Chinese class while the girls were at school during the day, then picked them up after school. I took the train to Tianjin when necessary, worked at the business, then took the train back to Beijing at night.

For me it was a rewarding time. My daughters learned Chinese, I helped RSP initiate many profitable projects in Tianjin, and these efforts put them on the map as an international design outlet. But after two years, Rene was ready to go home. We returned to Minnesota in 2008, just in time for Fourth of July fireworks.

From that point on, I became a contract employee for RSP, still holding the position of general manager for China, until 2018 when we finally closed the Tianjin office. By then we had fewer projects, and the requisite taxes had become a burden to the company. These taxes are cumbersome and often totally unrelated to the business. For example, RSP was paying housing taxes for employees when I was the only employee and lived in Minnesota. We paid environmental taxes for manufacturing cleanup even though we did no manufacturing. We even paid unemployment taxes without ever filing a claim.

Doing business in China can be a conundrum. There is the potential to sell Buicks and Audis, Coke, and Starbucks coffee. Smart, large retailers like Sam's Club, France's Carrefour, and Germany's Metro operated profitably in China for a long time. Yet challenges remain, with unpredictable explosives lying beneath the surface that must be navigated. A company can stay clean, above corruption and free of bribes and deceit. It is possible to sleep at night. But I have left money on the table many times. Once you go down the road of corruption in any way, they have you.

But the ultimate obstacle to doing business in China is overcoming the challenging "rule of the people." True laws are not upheld by a judiciary system; they are left to the whims of individuals who assume power. Too often someone is ready to reject, disapprove, revoke, or renege on a deal. And always with "good reason." But it is never the real reason. The real reason has to do with who and when, almost never what and why. During my years in business, I have heard:

- The person in charge is not available, is traveling, is at Party School, is anywhere else.
- The computer system is down.
- We cannot find the key to the drawer where the approval stamp is kept.
- There is no time slot available to schedule an approval meeting.
- The person who approved the project got transferred, or received a promotion or a demotion, or worse—went to jail or unexpectedly died.

Regardless I have conducted my business in China always aiming for the best, whatever that might be.

And then I return to a country where I have come to know once unimaginable luxuries. I can never forget how poor I was as a child. Even by Communist China standards, we were poor. My mother would pretend she had eaten to leave more for her children. People were hungry all the time. When the government finally allowed us to borrow against our next month's grain ration on the twenty-fifth of each month, long lines formed at five in the morning even though the store did not open until eight. We were destitute. And in this way, we were always borrowing ahead, always perpetuating our own need. The food allotted by the government barely sustained us.

I live a very different life now, and my children live a very different life. But it has been important to me that they know where I have been and how far I have journeyed. For that reason, I have taken my family back to visit Cheng Village several times over the years. We have always brought gifts, and I have always looked for familiar faces. On one of our trips, we brought ramen noodles, packets of candy bars like Snickers, peanut butter and other small gifts that were not easily obtainable in the countryside. As we were leaving, a woman approached me, bent over nearly in half so that I could not see her face. But as she neared, I recognized her. She was the one who had helped me wash and reconstruct my quilt.

It is hard to explain how dirty our clothing could get when we worked so hard and had to walk a quarter mile for water. People had to be practical. After I had lived through two winters on the farm, the quilt my mother made for me was so dirty, it felt like leather, and lice had begun to breed in it. But I did not know how to deconstruct it to separate the two outer layers from the disintegrating cotton inside.

This woman came forward to help me. Her husband was the village doctor, and she was well-regarded. She showed me how to wash the two outer cloths and dry them in the sun. She then guided me to gather bits of cotton from the fields, place them side by side carefully and smooth them to fit between the outer layers. She took time to show me the technique for poking holes into the cloth and stitching the quilt back together, then making rows of stitches back and forth diagonally to hold the layers in place. How could I ever forget that level of kindness?

Now in her sixties and hunched terribly, she greeted me and my family. We were at the end of our visit and had run out of gifts. But I could not leave without giving her something, so I took off my watch and offered it to her. That was the last time I saw her. I'll never forget the image of her familiar face looking up at me from her severely bent body, her joy at seeing me again and meeting my family.

I maintained relationships with the people of Cheng Village because they befriended me in that difficult time and because we have a shared humanity. Why didn't they get to have a better life? Who is to say they should have so little when others have so much? Most of the Chinese people I knew in my years there were good people. They worked hard against terrible odds. In the *hukou* system, they had no opportunity to move beyond their circumstances, to dream and strive and make a better life. The government had decided what their lives should be, and that was that. And even though the rules are now somewhat relaxed, the ceilings remain. The limitations remain. If you do not pass the college exam, you do not rise. If you do not have connections, you are not chosen. If you come from a remote village, your options are few. America, however, is a country built by many people born in humble or difficult situations who dream and work hard and change their lives forever.

I tell my story as a reminder of how it was for me then, how it remains for many people in many poor places around the world. I have deep gratitude for the freedoms I have known, the opportunities I have found, and the people who contributed to my good fortune. I have never stopped marveling at all that has happened. My father told me to "do great things," but if I accomplished anything great, it is largely because I had supportive parents, family, and friends, and the great fortune to be in the United States. I have given thanks every day since stepping foot in this extraordinary country.

MOVE MOUNTAINS

Amber Glassman

Whatever you do in life,
Do not settle for anything that dulls your spark.
Find your passion and pursue what sets your soul on fire.
Do not settle for a star when you deserve the galaxy.
Do not settle for a wave when you deserve the sea.
Do not settle for anything less.
Trust yourself.
Know your worth.
Don't just climb mountains.
Move them.

Afterword

Brian Tiehan Chang died at home in Prior Lake, Minnesota on September 19, 2023, surrounded by his wife Rene, his daughters Natalie and Melanie, and two of his three sisters, Tieying and Tiewei. He succumbed after a spirited fight against a rare cancer which had initially struck during the terrifying first months of the COVID-19 pandemic and returned after two years of remission.

Brian met this trial with all the determination and resourcefulness with which he had faced other daunting challenges in his life. The man with the gumption to study English on a collective farm during the Cultural Revolution never abandoned hope. He sought out the best medical care, rigorously followed his treatment and nutritional plans, and remained optimistic to the end despite experiencing often excruciating pain.

As always, Brian made every minute count. Following his diagnosis, he threw himself into writing this autobiography. And what a tale it is. At one level, it's a quintessentially American success story about a plucky newcomer who succeeds in the land of opportunity through hard work, self-belief, and ingenuity. At the same time, it's a multigenerational chronicle of self-sacrifice, resilience, and adaptation amid China's turbulent modern history. It's also Brian's effort to make sense of his own life and convey his gratitude, devotion and love to his family, friends and teachers on both sides of the Pacific.

In person, as on the page, Brian was an unusually gifted storyteller. Passionate and gregarious, he punctuated his stories with jokes or Chinese aphorisms that helped bring out their full meaning. He was open and unafraid to show emotion—he could laugh at himself, express gratitude, and shed tears. Brian, who often went to bed hungry as a boy, loved few things more than hosting joyous dinner parties at the Chang family home, where the conversation flowed over heaping plates of his delicious Chinese food and glasses of Cabernet Sauvignon or Chinese spirits.

And his life left him with a storehouse of experiences to share. It took him from a six-person, one-bedroom apartment in Tianjin with a communal kitchen and toilet, to his and Rene's dream home on a golf course with a lake view, wine cellar and pool table. Along the way, he saw much of the world—first as an employee of China's Railway Ministry and later as an international executive and keen tourist who earned over a million frequent flyer miles on one carrier alone—the equivalent of more than two roundtrips to the moon.

Brian's exceptionally eventful career also furnished him with rich material. He was a reluctant farmer under Mao who became a grain trader at Cargill. He was a high-flying financial analyst at both SoftBank and Alliance Capital who was too restless and entrepreneurial for corporate life and started and invested in multiple businesses. A model student who credited education as his ticket to a better life, Brian taught English in China, volunteered his time as a popular Chinese cooking instructor in Minnesota, and led seminars in an EMBA program in Taiwan. He also became a trusted guide to his birth and adopted countries, leading Chinese business delegations to the U.S. and American delegations to China, including that of then Minnesota Governor Jesse Ventura.

Added to this incomparable wealth of experiences, Brian's natural curiosity, love of language, and ability to strike up a conversation with just about anyone made him an especially compelling correspondent, as these pages make clear.

Nicknamed the 'Energizer Bunny,' Brian was on the move until the end. During a break from chemotherapy, he took one final trip to Asia with his daughter Melanie to visit his students in Taipei, pay his respects to his parents' graves near sacred Mount Taishan, and visit friends and family in Tianjin.

True to his buoyant personality, the last time we spoke, Brian conveyed gratitude and optimism about the care he was receiving. He even cracked a joke from his hospital bed, his eyes twinkling and his warm, familiar smile flashing briefly across his gaunt face.

This memoir is Brian's final gift to the world. It's an inspiring illustration of how far a person can travel, physically and metaphorically, in a single lifetime and an ode to hope in the face of adversity. Long may it keep his wonderful memory alive.

Adam Pillsbury

With Dave Janiszewski (top left), Kelly Lorix (top right),
Louann Bosmans (bottom left), and Peter Beck (bottom right)

Acknowledgments

I have been encouraged to write a book about my life for quite some time. Friends, colleagues, associates, and family members describe my life's story as compelling and inspirational. I have always felt honored and humbled by their remarks, but I believed only the famous and accomplished could write a book. I have finally heeded their sage advice!

In 2016, my longtime friend, *Peter Beck,* a renowned photographer, published a photo journal book featuring sixteen immigrants who came from all corners of the globe to settle in Minnesota. I was honored to be one of the immigrants featured in his book. Later, through Peter's book, *Christina MacGillivray,* a contract officer of the United Nations Human Rights Commission, contacted me for an interview about life as a Chinese immigrant in the U.S.

On a summer day in 2017 at my suburban Minneapolis home, Christina and I chatted for more than two and a half hours. This interview resulted in an animated video production, which she used to compile recorded manifestos of fifteen of us immigrants who left their motherlands in search of a better life in the United States. Christina and I have become good friends since our interview in 2017. She, too, encouraged me to write this book and was kind enough to send me the audio recordings of my interview, which laid the foundation for this book.

Still, writing a book is not an easy task. Like the saying goes about quitting smoking: to quit is easy; I have quit many times. I have started writing many times, but for various reasons, I have been unable to resume, let alone cross the finish line.

One silver lining for me emerged from the COVID-19 pandemic: idle time, which, prior to that, had been a rare commodity in my life, and provided the impetus to resume writing. Although many of the events took place decades ago, I remember them as if they happened last week. Penning the story of my mother dying in the hospital corridor was emotionally draining, as well as recollecting the day I was sent from Tianjin, where I was born and raised, to a farming village for the rest of my life. Reliving these experiences was both exhausting and cathartic.

I am truly grateful for my writing partner, *Kathleen Novak*. She and I spent hundreds of hours together and individually to get this book written, organized, and edited. Her contribution has been indispensable.

I feel indebted to so many who have enriched my life journey. The phrase "thank you" is wholly inadequate to express my heavy debt of gratitude.

In addition, I would be remiss not to recognize the following people:

André and *Melanie Gillet*. André and I met in the Summer of 1979 in Guangzhou. I met Melanie, André's beautiful, kind, and loving wife, when they welcomed me at the airport in

With André and Melanie Gillet

1984 when I arrived in Minnesota. The Gillets became my surrogate parents who not only offered a safe haven but presented me with amazing opportunities. Melanie Gillet was such an amazing lady that we named our daughter, Melanie, after her.

Roland and Rachel Fischer. I met the Fischers in 1983 when they were teaching English at Nankai University in Tianjin, China. The Fischers affectionately call me their "Chinese son." I am honored to call them my American parents.

Jesse Parker and Amy Kahn. Jesse Parker was my English teacher when I was a sophomore at Changsha Railway College. I met Amy Kahn, Jesse's wife, in 1986, when I visited them in their Boston home. Nine years later, Rene and I were engaged at the Parker/Kahn beach "shack" in Martha's Vineyard!

Tierong, Tiewei, Cary Humphries, Tieying, and Brian in 1996.

Cary and Margot Humphries. Cary and I met on my first day of work at Cargill. Cary was president of Cargill North America. I was a management trainee, which was an unlikely, though serendipitous way to begin a life-long friendship. Cary is the most devout Christian I have ever met and is instrumental in my journey to discovering a loving God.

Dave and Janet Janiszewski. Dave and I met in the winter of 1985, when we shared a dorm room at the University of Minnesota. Dave taught me a great deal about what America is all about: working hard, playing hard, preserving individualism, and contributing to societal well-being. I visited them when they gave birth to all three of their children (who are grown now!), and I am the proud godfather to Grace, their youngest.

Adam and Judy Pillsbury. Adam and I met through André Gillet's son-in-law, John Bean, who happened to work at a wealth management company. Adam was one of my groomsmen at our wedding in 1996. He and Judy lived in Beijing from 1998 to 2018, where both of their daughters were born. When I served as China General Manager of RSP Architects, they were our neighbors in Beijing. Adam was editor-in-chief of *That's Beijing*, a weekly magazine catering to expatriates living in China. Adam's linguistic talent and editorial expertise have tremendously enriched this book.

Kai Dong. My best middle school and high school friend. We live in two different countries and two different worlds. However, our half-century-plus long friendship remains steadfast.

Louann Koopmeiners Bosmans. My BFF in graduate school and beyond, who is the embodiment of kindness and grace. Words are inadequate to express my gratitude for all she has done for me.

Tieying, Tierong, and *Tiewei Zhang.* My sisters who have supported me and were there for me so many times in my life.

There are countless additional friends and family worthy of mention, so I beg their forgiveness in advance for not naming everyone. You know who you are, and I thank you from the bottom of my heart!

I am eternally grateful to all the people who helped me celebrate life's milestones and navigate life's challenges.

www.ingramcontent.com/pod-product-compliance
Lightning Source LLC
Chambersburg PA
CBHW041722070526
44585CB00001B/2